"Little boy lost".
My journey
Adam Stuart Pick.

Recognitions & Thanks to:

Rachel Studley, for being a Brilliant Friend over the past few years. I won't forget that, thanks a bunch mate.

Thanks to Network for change for the excellent support since 2002, thanks to Clare Hill and Shaun Johnston for their support, and advice in this venture.

Thanks to Corrin Desborough and Chaz ram from the Llgbc, in Leicester for years of support, opportunities, and the knowledge that I am valued.
Thanks to everyone on the www.madnotbad.co.uk forum

Thanks to my cell, and my church for the support I have gotten since November 2005

Thanks to everyone else who assisted and supported me during the past five years. It means so much more to me than I can say. You all know who you are.

Hello. My name is Adam, and I decided to write a book to explore some issues within my life, to promote healing and recovery, both in myself and others. I have been very confused about my sexuality for a very long time, I think I was about 12 when I first realized I wasn't like other boys. It took far longer until I was able to pin down the difference. This occurred in about 2001. As important as my sexuality is however, that is just a part of me, and there are other issues I will address here, as I attempt to find myself, well and truly.

This book is aimed at both service users, and those who want to get a better idea of the kind of things those who suffer mental distress face. In this book, are personal experiences, both written at the time, and full of emotion, and those written after the fact, and maybe more logical? Both give an accurate flavor as to how I cope and feel much of the time. There are also opinion pieces, some social commentary, explorations in to self harm, feeling suicidal, depression and personality disorder, all of which I have much experience. This book is very much a journey of discovery. I would be more than happy for you to accompany me on this journey, an exploration of self, an attempt by me to come to terms with myself, who I am, and to gain some direction in my life. This book was written when suicide seemed the only real option, the only way for me to escape a life that seemed unlivable. As such there will be many instances of dark thinking.

 I apologize in advance for any upset I may cause to anyone. I have spoken from my heart about how I feel, how I have been affected. I of course realize this in turn will affect others. This is not intended to jeopardize my relationships. Indeed, it's a purge for me. Indeed it is meant to let go of the negative and embrace the positive. This book is after all an exploration of my deepest thoughts and feelings. I mean no offense. There are no chapters, no divisions, as it is a flowing and natural progression of my thoughts and feelings, written as I was experiencing the emotion of the day, an organic process, and as such may deviate from the traditional book writing process. I hope this does not dampen your interest. Are you interested in getting to know the real me? Then read on.

I can seem different on different days. Sometimes I am logical, sensible, fully integrated into my day, certain of life, and my desire to live it, at other times I hallucinate and hear voices, I fear strange things and can appear over sensitive and strange. Reality shifts in and out, and I am not at peace at myself. In these instances I appear "crazy".

Today, I am "crazy". It comes and goes you see, this pesky strangeness. Psychosis they call it. It is such a pretty word for such an ugly thing. I shall attempt to make sense, although I offer you no guarantees. Actually, yes I do. Promise to make sense. Just not in this chapter. Have you ever felt a little crazy? Not pencils up your nose, growling and chasing people around on all fours crazy, but subtly different, feeling like you want to run away going agog, and wibbling quietly in the corner hiding beneath your invisible elephant? I have. In my case the elephant isn't an elephant, I'm not quite sure what it is, but its something, it's big and it means I don't see people the way they see each other. I am a freak. I am odd. Sometimes I see things, hear things, I have panic attacks:

great big horrible goblins of a thing, which sneak up behind me, twang my pant elastic and send me screaming up the road. They are not pleasant. Imagine your breath feeling superheated, your stomach feeling like its expanding your head feeling like two strongmen are trying to cave it in, your feet feeling they are made out of some alien substance and wishing for death, and you might have a slight idea how it feels. Seriously, it is not a pleasant phenomenon. I should know I have them. And I also feel crazy. I look crazy too, bulging eyes and short purple hair, hulking forehead and a look about the eyes which will probably send you into hysterics, or cause pant wetting fear. Depends on your personality, and whether or not I remembered to get dressed this morning.

You think I am kidding? I probably am. I actually don't know you see. Did I tell you I am odd? Good. Coz I am, obviously. My brain works in an oddly circular fashion, that's when it works at all. Know what I mean? Of course you don't. You are sane. Aren't you? If your not, I apologize. But if you happen to be sane, so am I, most of the time, surprisingly. Just not at this moment. I feel a bit of a reject. Just refuse. I am only Society's unwanted detritus. The world moves on as I hide under my duvet, night turns to day, and back again and I have not moved an inch. I think a week may have passed. Or it might be just a few days. Either way the world is turning. People are making a living whilst I decompose slowly. It is a brave new world. Oh yes, it is a brave new world. And my brain has decided to make sense for now. Wahoo.

It's a brave new world. It is a realm of endless possibilities. It is a place where anything is possible.

It is full of the bright young things and the heroes and architects of the future. The poets the writers and the musicians the politicians and the business men, the bold and the beautiful. Cultured gargantuan and spiritual masters. A fine place to live in. or is it? Depends on your perspective. If you are one of these artistic and talented folk, then the world is your oyster. If you are like me however…then it appears that the future isn't nearly so bright and sparkly.

I am a bear. A great shaggy haired, lumbering beast, unshaved, unwashed, uncultured, in a word consisting of talented folk. The fab five, fashion designers, foodies, wine connoisseurs, musicians, writers, art critics, and other luminaries of the modern world – I feel somewhat sad and outmoded.

I feel unwise in a world full of gurus, spiritually awakened and generally enlightened folk. You only have to look around to find your Buddhist practitioners, your students of fengshui, and I feel slightly inferior, due to the fact that I am, in short, the most spiritually unaware, unfocussed slob I have ever met. I haven't got a clue when it comes to chakra points, and which aromatherapy oils work for what, and tofu? Can't stand the stuff!

I am one of the great unwashed, a great shaggy haired lumbering beast, unshaved, un-washed, uncultured. A social miss-fit who feasts on burgers kebabs, reads sci-fi and is addicted to star gate sg1. Nope, a more inapt and uncool, uncouth, maladapted person you shall not meet. So when your talented, cool, looking, cool acting socially successful free spirits confront me, I just want the earth to open up and swallow me, you know? I look like a yob; (which I am, surprisingly, just an intelligent and sensitive yob).

I look like I probably couldn't even spell culture, (which I can't, being dyslexic… wonderful thing, spellcheckers.) yet alone participate in the practicing of it! I watch the tai-chi practicing, tofu eating, (I have no idea how they do that, it's bloody awful stuff) Soya milk drinking folk, as they practice their yoga, and ponder spiritual matters, and I think, why you? Why not me? I admit here is more than a slight tinge of jealousy going on here. Bloody shiny happy people. Grr. Not happy. Not happy at all. I think I may vomit in protest, in fact.

I see the writers, the musicians, the entrepanuers, the entertainers, the young chefs, the wits, the comedians, the political next best things, the poets, and other generally talented folk. (Letting their wondrous talent shine all over the place, making me look a tad shabby). There they all are, hanging out in their cool bars, with their saxophones by their feet, their guitars and clarinets resting against the wall, their laptops whirring gently, their recently published books of poems and philosophy on the tables, eating fancy foods and looking cool.

And I just want to curl up and disappear. I am so bloody embarrassed to be me, to even be in the same room as these amazing, shiny, talented people, with their wit, and fantastic hair, smart clothes, and looks tom cruise would die for. Unable to handle the embarrassment any longer, I bow my head and I shuffle off, amazed that I even had the ordacity to be anywhere near these, luminous beings. Watching as they start creating new works, and changing the world for the better, gleefully, all over the place….

What the hell is wrong with this picture? Apart from the fact I am wearing grey sweat pants and a jumper with mayonnaise and curry sauce down the front? They even smell better than I do. I think I need to start trying to smarten myself up a bit. What do you reckon? Maybe even go as far as having a shave once a week, or something. No seriously, there is somewhat of a ravine between how they are, what they can do, and me, little old I. I feel superfluous, a redundancy, just a spare part, a cog in a machine that doesn't need me.

It is indeed, somewhat disconcerting to see someone who is the same age as me, living a life of good food, interesting lectures, an intellect the size of the empire states building, and then, contrast them against the socially unaware, culturally bankrupt, intellectually barren wreck which is me.

Time to crawl back into the pit, from whence I came, and fantasize I have the body of vin-deisel, the face of tom cruise, the intelligence and wit of Steven fry, the tan of dale Winton, and the talent of George Orwell. (I am kidding about the tan of Dale Winton, obviously).Then I would be more equipped to deal with a world full of up and comers, and I wouldn't feel as much of a societal reject, a malformed, maladaptive recluse –

A hermit, a refugee, stuck on an island named "hopeless". Let's face it; lets look at the ugly (and rather pathetic) state of my life, and we shall see the truth of the matter. I have no career prospects, no fountain of knowledge with which to impress my friends, and as for culture, and knowledge of food? I don't even know which side my knife and fork should be on, and cant even spell geography, let alone be able to tell you where countries are, and the cultures of their peoples.

That's it, I am washed up, at the age of 26, and I am passé, old hat, an eccentricity in a smooth fast placed world of businessmen and politicians. I am destined to fall by the wayside, only to be trampled upon by those rushing past, headlong into their great future.

So I watch the architects of the future, in the sun, from over the other side of the street, in shadow, and rain, wondering what the future has in store for talent less miss-fits like me. As I have started, I might as well give you a real insight into how I look, because that might give way to imagining how I feel, and this can only lead to knowing me a bit, surely? I am a pretty average looking fellow really. If you can get past the dirty, unkempt mass of hair that balances upon my head, like a sheep on some dessert island.

What else is there to tell you? I am a heavy set kinda guy, not small, about five ft 10, green/blue eyes. I possess hair that can seem to vary color from day to day. Red, purple, blue or black hair, depending on the mood I am in, really, clothes wise, the past few months has seen a change in how I am comfortable. It used to be baggy jeans, now its combats, dark colors, black green, blue, thick grungy jumpers and cardigans (my favorite is a black chunky nit cardy with a hood, and I love it to bits).

 I wear black skate trainers; sometimes I wear a blue blazer or blue long length denim over my hoody. I quite like the gothic look, and even though I like that type music (Bauhaus, etc. I will speak about my music tastes later on, at some-point)) and relate to the attitude somewhat, I wouldn't feel comfortable dressed that way. I guess the truth is that I don't feel a need to truly stand out visually; I want to do that by my actions, and my mind, sort of. But I both like and admire that out there type look. True individualism is a wonderful thing. Although I wonder if any of us is that, truly individual. I have no piercing or tattoos, though that's only a matter of time. I want tribal/Celtic tats on my arms, back, legs, maybe my neck. Whenever I see pic's of these types of tat, I feel drawn and pulled by them; they really mean something to me, kind of a journey, trying to discover myself. Strange I know but true. Its Celtic heritage type stuff, I guess. I always felt I liked the Celts better than my own Brethren, which is odd, I know.

So, there you have it, I am a big lumbering shaggy haired oaf, who likes the whole post punk/ new metal, colored hair thang. I am a natural pessimist. I focus on the black, then deciding it's not black enough, I go deeper, spoiling an otherwise lovely day with the blackness of my thinking. Daft I know, but there you are.These thoughts lead to others, of a darker, and more morderlin nature, but I endeavour to write as I find, as I see, as I am. A true representation of me as a person exists on these pages, an attempt to share my essence, my chi, to allow others to see me as I see myself, and an attempt to some how find the meaning in my life, by exploring the words I write. Thus I hope to find out just who I "AM" –

To find the soul that must dwell behind my eyes, somewhere. But there, I am not alone, and in this at least, I find comfort. Many of my fellows search for meaning, and that search takes many guises. Existentialism, Buddhism, Jainism, Confucianism, Marxism, politically based, philosophically based, or even religion based.

There is still an ongoing quest for what matters, and makes sense for each of us. Knowing this however, doesn't make the journey any damn easier, I say, with a wry smile. I am so anxious and frightened, I feel as if my heart is going to implode, and kill me, as melodramatic as that sounds. I feel as if everyone is talking about me and making horrendous judgements about my character, judging me and deciding that I am guilty of some crime… when all that I am guilty of is being extremely insecure and scared…

And it is true I do have a temper problem, but this is aimed at myself, thinking that I am thick worthless and stupid, a nobody, a nothing…. and I get mad if I think people aren't understanding me, or judging me harshly, these things do make me mad, and it is true that when I get angry I cannot control the intensity of the anger… but I am very rarely angry in the first place.

I feel as if people are looking down on me, the way I dress, the way I look, the way I speak, the things I do. As if nothing is good enough, as if I am dirt under their feet. Talk about having a chip on your shoulder. I've got the whole bloody potato field. It isn't enough that I feel useless, stupid, thick, pathetic, it seems to me that people think the same, even though they say this isn't the case.

No matter how hard I try, I am never good enough; I just don't understand some things. I get confused, and don't always get what people mean. Colloquialisms confuse me, slang baffles me, and people often seem amused by my blank stare. I look and act dumb, and show my ignorance with every word I utter…

And this is of great embarrassment to me. I find it hard to concentrate, and as I am so literal, things fall into black or white. It is a simple thing. It is nothing more and nothing less. Shades of grey to me are just abstract concepts, not actual existing facts, a nebulous region of confusion and lack of logical sense, and this is perhaps my biggest failing, I know not. It is somewhat strange is this phenomenon... Others thrive, whilst I stumble. I need to overcome my pre-disposition to try and analyse everything down to its smallest constituent part… once I have somehow achieved this, I will be able to throw of the shackles of my mind, and move on into the light, perhaps…

But that is not easy. It has been a survival mechanism, a means to live. But it's faulty and causes me more suffering than I can endure these days. I am sick and tired of feeling so inadequate and inept, so lowly small and unimportant. I feel as if people look down on me, because I give them no other option. I do nothing worthy of respect, every good thing I have, I have been given, every thing I have done, has not been my own hand. No. I've been assisted and aided in, and allowed to do these things. None of this has been my own achievement.

I have done nothing of my own merit for the past 7 years or so – I am truly a failure…. At this point, I feel the need to tell you I do not want sympathy. Well, yeah, guess I do. But don't pity me; else I shall hang you upside down by your ankles until all your change falls out your pockets. And I will give you a wedgy. Well, figuratively speaking. I do not want you to go wa-wa over this. I am only saying it how it is. I am merely stating facts. By this I mean that I have done things, yes, but not alone.

Opportunities have been handed to me on a plate, and I have capitalised on said opportunities… but I have not earned my own shot at anything. And that knowledge ways heavily on my tired mind. Of course it does, I have done nothing worth my salt, and my ego won't stand for it. They are bloody male hormones. They suck. It is nasty.

And I feel so hurt by everything, a glance, a word, and my heart is in pieces, my spirit crushed. What is wrong with me? Why am I so bloody pathetic? I feel like I am an emotional wreck, lost out at sea. I am Unable to pick myself up, shake myself, forge on, and succeed. Why am I unable to do a simple thing like bloody well get a grip, and conquer my fear? I used to have that capacity, and maybe, just maybe, it still dwells inside? Why am I full of all this anger? It is a bloody travesty, that's what it is mate.

 Why do I feel like crying every second? Why do I hurt this much? The sensation is like being skinned alive, and wrapped in salt, and shrink-wrapped, preserved forever in a cocoon of pain. Well, Probably.

Maybe it's something I have to go through, (not being wrapped in salt and shrink wrapped, obviously) these growing pains. And this is all the trauma of a mind growing and stretching, learning, and flowing. Flowing and shifting as I shed my own metaphysical skin and evolve into a new me. A form that is a previously unknown one a new state – An update on the old model. Adam revisited perhaps? I seem to be thinking strange thoughts… (And talking utter rubbish, don't think I haven't noticed.) But this is not in itself, a bad thing. Indeed. It could be part of my evolution, into a better, more thoughtful me…

I can only hope that this is the case. Either that or I am just crazy, and in danger of starting acting odder than I do now, and eating old pieces of cardboard in a dank basement corner somewhere.. Who can say? Wow. This is tiring. The ramblings of a crazy man, translated to paper. Sitting here, looking out of the window, gazing down into the street, I find myself watching the people walking by, caught up in their lives, trapped by the marching onwards of time. And with a sudden lurch, I am thrown backwards and into my past, as if in some strange warping of time, echoes of laughter and mirth reverberating within my psyche, memories of Adventures and escapades vying with one another, fighting for dominance, repeating over and over,

Like a decaying signal, losing power as it travels through the air. At first it is strong and clear. Then more distant, as if it is corrupted and fading into static. White noise and ambient sound, pressing and pushing against the walls of my mind, trying to burst open my head like some exotic fruit, leaving its core exposed, left to rot and decompose. Now my mind is like the waterways of Venice, my thoughts like gondolas, matrices of thought and desire, flowing as if water, under the bridge of intellect and out of my consciousness,

Only to be repeated in the future. Much like an echo of an echo, a memory of a memory, corrupted and withered, no longer a true image of the past, but a mere representation, now a flicker of what could have, what might have been. Perhaps what still could be, far into the future? The sounds loop around each other, merging and becoming one, until this is all I can hear, all I can perceive, sight failing, touch now unreal.

Smell and taste confused, almost as if I can both taste and smell sound itself. I cannot escape this cage, this crystalline and precious prison, for it is one of my own making, This is mutiny damn it! My senses are seizing control. My unconsciousness is conspiring to destroy my conscious, so that I am only a ghost, a memory of the past, haunting the present, and wanting only to be a valid part of the future. A spectre, watching as the future unfolds, in its glory, its pulsating brilliance, bursting forwards, drowning out my own presence. Deleting all traces of my weak signal, as it decays, making me even more unreal, until like the setting of the sun, I am gone, forever.

This leads me to ask the burning question... Am I real, do I exist? WHO AM I? What is my purpose? For what purpose am I here, for what cosmic reason, do I exist. Dreams come all the time, but they never seem to go, as if my spirit is a storage battery, and one that is beginning to leak. Day and night they parade within my head, they are always with me, floating just beyond my eyelids - if you look into my eyes, what would you see? Would you see Adam, would you glimpse my soul?

If you were to photograph me, would you see me, or a collection of thoughts and experiences? Just a cacophony of sounds and images, would you see only a never-ending whirlwind of thoughts, images, memory of past times, glimpses of the future, would you see a person, or merely a glimpse of what used to be a person, but is no more? Just the random firing of electrical impulses firing within a cerebrum. And now I can almost feel those electrical impulses failing, my mind begins to fade, fading from loud, active vibrant, strong and powerful, roaring, dropping in tone and pitch, to weak, frail silent, whimpering, dead.

My heartbeat bangs and pounds within me, sounding throughout my entire being, the blood boiling in my veins, as it pulses manically around my frail form. These feelings are intensifying now. I can feel every inhale and exhale I make, and I can feel the neurons in my brain, actually feel the electrical impulses fire, struggling pathetically, to keep me going, keep this life from flitting away, into the darkness, forever.

And in this time, in this space, I can see everything, and with a clarity that burns me, and reduces me to ashes. Some thoughts are too vivid, too bright, fiery and massive for a merely human mind to hold, and they cast confused glimpses into what lays beyond, beyond the realm of the physical, beyond the realm of the mental, and into a place of pure energy, where time and space are but concepts, a place where there is nothing, and everything, at the same time.

At times like this, it is as if I can hear the call of the universe, the birth cry of life itself, for we are but the blink of creations eye, one step in the evolution of something greater than we. I do seem to perceive the world rather differently than my fellows, and this disturbs me greatly. I know we are all different from each other…. but then I think I am different again, above and beyond that….

I have come to the conclusion that I do not perceive the world correctly. I don't see beauty in anything, I no longer seem to appreciate taste, or truly like the smell of something, or hear a nice sound… it seems that my ability to perceive these things has diminished… maybe this is a function of being depressed, but maybe its something more, a flaw in my very makeup, a fault that prevents me from truly being alive….

For if you can't exist in the moment, and appreciate a beautiful thing then you aren't alive are you? Your heart is not open, and your spirit does not sing. You don't see the value in other life… This is where I find myself, alive and yet not so. I think that beauty is a mental image, that is, something that does not exist physically in the world, its cognition, a mere function of the brain, something to do with the way our brains perceive and interpret data. A flower isn't beautiful, it is just a flower; it's our brains that overlay emotional responses to an object that makes them nice, pretty, whatever. They are not of themselves pretty… that's why some people think flowers are nice, and others don't, some people find certain people attractive others don't, because there is no such thing as beauty outside of the cerebellum, outside of perception.

Most people are able to look at an object, or person, and find them attractive, the mind interprets what it is seeing, an emotion response is attached, and that person observes that such and such is beautiful. Alas, this seems not to be the case for me. I lack this mental set up. I think I rob the object of its beauty, like a physic vampire, draining the vitality from the living, or rather that I am unable to perceive it, cannot perceive it in the way others can. I seem to break an image down into metaphor, instead of seeing a flower; I see a collection of thoughts. This is the truth, as odd as this may seem. I see the flower only as a representation of data, I interpret what I see and analyze it so much that the actual image is lost behind a veil of thought, in this way I rob the flower of its beauty.

I do the same with conversation, somebody will say something, I will take that, focus on the words, and how they are placed together, and focus on the structure. I will read into that my own meanings, and re-interpret what has been said, so that the original meaning, the truth behind the words, the feelings that the person attached to them the deep expression of the way they see the world, it is all lost. The beauty of their words is lost, the expression, the essence of their spirit is removed, and so the words become meaningless, empty, and cold. I can see this happening and yet cannot change it and stop this tragedy from occurring.

And this is what I do with everything, analyse, interpret, reinterpret, draining each thing, each interaction, each observation of its fundamental energy, until nothing remains, but an empty husk. I learnt the gift of analysing through therapy, in the hope that I would understand myself, and my actions, and how they impacted upon others, provoking their responses to me, a positive, but steep learning curve, one destined to carry me out of the towering inferno, alive, and free.

But somehow, it became a curse, and life itself seems to have lost its lustre, as if gold plated, losing its shiny exterior, only to reveal the rust below it. What I know as life seems sucked me within itself, taking me into an alternate dimension of confusion. A place of Mishmashed concepts, edited, cut, and slammed together, until up is down, right is left, and I am abandoned to my fate. And so the world I live in, the mental place in which I reside is cold, without warmth, without meaning. I do not understand everyday interactions. I do not connect with the warmth, that being with other human beings provides.

I do not feel the connection, the interconnectivity that binds each living person to each living person. I do not live in the moment; I do not live, for I analyze everything to the nth degree, until any meaning is lost. It is in this way I confound and confuse myself, because I become lost in thought, so entrenched, I do not know how I arrived at this point. I cannot see the ending, I cannot remember the beginning. I know only where I am now, lost in a jumble of metaphors, half composed thoughts, and lost in a forest of sounds and images…

And I try how I try. I strive so hard to understand, to see the meaning behind speech and images, behind events, that I miss a wealth of information. I do not truly taste the orange, or truly see the colour blue, because I am so lost in my own thoughts, I can't truly appreciate these things for what they are. I am so introverted, I don't see the life in others, I don't appreciate the beauty of a sunset, and I find that I cannot appreciate a bird's song. Even something that simple, passes me by, as does all beauty, all things that can touch a human heart. Of course I cant, these things are in the real world, and I reside in my head, so I miss life. In this way I exist, but don't live. In this way, my heart is cold, my heart, is stone.

I feel such remorse and sadness that I am missing these things. My capacity for regret seems endless, cavernous, with no end in sight. I feel so empty and soulless, as if my spirit has died, my essence has spilled out on the cold concrete floor, only to be absorbed and drawn into the earth. Or perhaps, evaporating, becoming vapour, and travelling up into the heavens. This thought provides cold comfort. I feel cold.

I walk in a daze, not truly seeing, not truly hearing, not truly a person at all. Merely an echo of what was an echo of life, a leftover, a walking corpse. I take no pleasure in anything, I understand little, I know only that I am lost, and am desperate to find myself once more; I want to recapture the feeling of being alive. I want to be valid, I need purpose, and I need direction.

Surely my life must have purpose, reason, the human body, as wondrous as it is, so perfect, yet so vulnerable, fragile, surely evolution would not have provided us this, for no reason? Why have we alone, out of all the countless forms of life, why have we, developed further than the rest? Why would the holy books, the Koran, the torah, the bible, and many others, decree that suicide was a sin, not to be countanced, and if you did choose death, that you would be cast off before god. Why would they say this if there was not a supreme, deep meaning, to each and every human life?

I can accept we might not be devolved enough emotionally, and intellectually for us to understand its meaning, but surely, its there? It is waiting for us, to discover and embrace it? Monks and Spiritualists. People of all faiths, creeds, religions. Occasionally glimpsing the overwhelming truth behind existence? And unlike Douglas Adam's suggests, I am pretty sure the meaning to life, the universe and everything, is not forty two! Have to say though, I love his books, and find his wit, his wry humour, and his humanity, refreshing. Him, I admire. Whilst I am on the subject, of people I admire… there are a few others I feel I should share with you. It may give us both an insight into my physke.

People I most Admire

I admire true individuals who don't try and appear different; they don't go out of their way to show how different they are, because it's obvious. It is part of them. They think differently. It shows by their actions, not words. They aren't Clones of everybody else, they aren't sheep, but they don't feel a need to go out and prove it to all and sundry, either. People like:

Stephen Fry, Robert Smith, (both struggled with depression, suicidal tendencies, both have brilliant minds, distinct personalities, quiet dignity, and pride, as well as great wit, intelligence, And courage, and both have made a huge impact on Certain groups in society) Billy Connolly, Dylan Moran (for being so funny, and spot on when it comes to society – I agree with them, wholeheartedly, both the irrelevant bits, and the darker world view)

Sir Steven Redgrave (for overcoming so many health difficulties to achieve all he did – so many gold medals – and he is still making a living, with dignity. The strength of his character is unbelievable).

Another is the fantastic Dr Stephen Hawkins (such a mind, brilliant, brave, courageous, living in a crippled body, but still bright, unique, special.) They are all role models for me, and I try to remember them, when times get tough. I want to be different, yes, unique, but above all I want to be me, myself, and behave with dignity, respect, I want to be courageous, and possess quiet pride. But being courageous, and having dignity is quite hard to achieve, when you find you can't live your life, the way you want, because confusion, depression, anger, all gets in the way.

Life is all about the simple things I believe, and, I find the simple things in life almost impossible. Eating breakfast, or indeed any other meal, drinking, and bathing, the simple staples of life, are so, so difficult for me. All of these, they are indeed, the essentials to a decent, healthy state of being, and all of them, they are beyond me. Going outside for a simple walk is almost beyond me….and so I am barely existing, in the physical sense, but not truly living in the fullest sense of the word. There is a difference between the two I find. If you are alive you are fully participating in the moment. And I am not, just going through the motions, not in touch with life… Getting up, out of bed, leaving bed just to sit? This I find I cannot do…

If I have a reason to be out, i.e. a group or an organised activity, I can do it, at a stretch, at a push. But I hate it. Hate being pulled into the light, when I am at my most comfortable in the dark. In the dark I am safe, or at least, safer, potentially, than I am in the light. The light burns, socialising can damage the unaware, but then again, so can endless isolation. I say I resent it, but I also long for the release, the gift of true life. I want to participate and live. I want to get meaning from every day interactions. But if I am alone, I seem to be stuck; trapped in a spider's web of regret, in so far as I feel unsafe unless I am in bed…

We know this is depression of course, rearing its ugly, scaly head, trailing blood and pus everywhere. (This is my own vision of depression, a great black dragon, with fiery eyes, trailing blood and shadow). And this is no way to live. I admit I am depressed, and severely so, I try to see tomorrow, I try to see the future, but all I can see is sorrow. When the doctors the nurses and the psychiatrists seem to be judging you, making decisions on the basis of half baked observations this can have a rather bad affect on your mood. This ironically is what they look for, and it becomes a nasty circle. There is unfortunately a huge they and we culture, in Britain, but not it is admittedly, not as bad as it was. This is due to the hard work of professionals and service users working together throughout the country. But stigma is there, rearing its ugly head, they mistrust us it seems. Are scared if us and what we might do. But what causes them to mistrust us? Stigma of course… What causes us to hate the professionals, mistrusting and feeling resentful towards them? It is the same thing. It is Stigma.

I can't tell you how bloody sick and tired of the whole flaming thing. I am. I am sick of the stigma I have faced, being told I am not compliant, that I am over emotional, melodramatic, manipulative, and various others by people who don't bother to look at the situation I was in, the factors behind it, or even try to get to know me first, not really know me. They just see my diagnosis of BPD and stigmatize me. This pissed me off greatly though now I feel by hard work I have begun to educate those who are around me as to how I really am, and they don't do it as much. But Stigma is a huge bugbear with me, I just can't abide it and I have sworn to fight it wherever I find it, in whatever form I find it. This is precisely one of the reasons I decided to become a trainer. I did an adult teaching qualification to allow me to do this, and have never really looked back.

I have been a service user trainer for nearly three years now, fairly solidly, with the past six months off, attempting to sort out the foundations of my life before I returned to that way of life. It has been most thought precooking, exposing me to many different types of people and schools of thoughts, progressive ways of thinking, and some rather primitive and old fashioned stereotypical judgments that made my heart absolutely sink. As a 23 year old, I knew I wanted to make a difference, wanted to understand my diagnosis, I wanted to be heard, not shut down at every opportunity, I wanted to understand how I felt myself, I wanted to help others and I wanted to be a part of something. Over time, as I progressed, and got better and better at training, my focus changed somewhat, it wasn't about me, or feeling better, it was about educating others as to how they made me feel, and how they might make other service users feel.

And how I felt we could avoid the "them and us" culture between service users and the professionals who wanted to help us. As such I spoke about a wide range of subjects, ranging from my own diagnosis, BPD, which by this time I understood very well, as well as the other personality disorder types. I spoke about self harm, as a self harmer I knew a lot, and had insights into the motivations of other harmers, I spoke about the recover model, which isn't really a model, rather a way of viewing life, and person centered planning, both of which I have had in depth training in recently. I spoke about my own experiences of psychosis, voice hearing and much more, during my time with the plus group. I have led five or six workshops as well as done many talks in the past few years, and I am proud that we seem to have made people think. And that's what we need. We need to make people stop and think and reconsider prejudices and judgmental thinking.

We spoke to CPN's and junior nurses, doctors, all sorts. OT's the lot really. I was part of a two service user – two clinician team who delivered two eight week training courses, resulting in a total of 16 weeks of personality disorder basic awareness training, as part of the national framework, in partnership with NIMHE. Stigma was a huge issue and still is, and the heart of why I do what I do is simply, that I want to break down the barriers between people. I want us all to co-exist as people. Not labels, not diagnosis, none of that. If clinicians' see us as people who need support and we see them as people who, even though they feel helpless and frustrated sometimes, they really do care and are trying to help.

Its just a rather unpleasant fact, that both clinicians and users alike are institutionalized, trapped into limited ways of thinking by training, and do not really consider attempting to think outside of the box. Suspicion and judgmental behavior is what keeps us where we are. Hopefully the MH services will continue to expand into the community, units will close, and we will all co-exist in a more natural and holistic way. This is my vision for the future, and I know I share it with many others. We as service users do not always help ourselves when we kick off, shouting, crying, and behaving in certain ways. But the important thing to bear in mind I feel is that clinician's do no always help when they provoke this by making us feel they do not see or hear us, either. There needs to be a vast improvement in training and a restructuring of the system, all over the UK there are indictor's that people realize this and want to change the status quo, and bring everyone together, and I really do think people are starting to listen to each other, professional and user alike.

Things are still pretty damn bad in places, but things are changing. I believe this. When every mental health practioners has someone in their team, a colleague has suffered mental distress, and is open about it, we will know things have improved for the better. I know there is risk with this, I am aware of the many come backs and misgivings people have, such as we might have our own issues brought up, and it might be hard to cope with. Of course it is, as a mental health service user-trainer I find this almost everytime I speak, but with training and supervision these can be channeled into empathy, an ability to understand to an extent what others are going through, as you have been through similar yourself. There is a danger you might relate to the point it brings you down, or you give too much of yourself, but training supervision, internal counseling can address all of this. And yes, of course there are risks.

Everyday when we cross a road, there are risks. But do we stay home? No of course not. We are beset by crude and ancient ways of seeing things. A holistic way of dealing with issues, breaking down the barriers which segregate us, is the only way to make the world deal with issues in a more positive way. So let's take risks. True growth has to include risk. That is my opinion. Of course, it's only that, but I think its one shared by thousands, service user and clinician alike. I suffer from clinical depression and BPD alike. I have stated why I got into BPD training already, but Talking about BPD in depth would take a whole other book (and I may one day endeavor to write one, from a wholly service user perspective, but not today) so I will leave that for another to deal with. (There is lots of free excellent info, especially online if this is what you want) but Clinical Depression.

I would like to share how I feel, have to cope with it. And how I am sure others must sometimes feel also. So let's think about it shall we? Depression is such a pretty word for something so damn ugly. A lot of us get depressed, clinically depressed, where every effort to get out of bed is wasted, where every day roles into the next and each breath seems to be nothing but a torturous exercise in futility. Life seems pointless, as if it has no inherent meaning, and you are too down to look for its purpose. And it isn't a matter of just being able to pull yourself together is it? Is it, really?

If it were only that simple, there wouldn't be any depressives out there. We don't choose it, it's not cool, and it's foolish to think otherwise. It's not about being "a little bit down" or a "little under the whether" its not oh my favourite radio show has been cancelled oh well' Nothing so easy for us. Instead of that its: "I cannot live my life. It will never get better. I might as well end it now". At least that's how it's been for me. What I am trying to say is there is a million miles between merely being down and clinical depression. It's not an easy one to deal with. Talking from my own experience here, it is like carrying the weight of the world upon your shoulders. And if like me, you are paranoid with it, every strange person is an enemy, behind every street corner; a horror awaits you – its unliveable, its horrible, a living nightmare.

I suffered this, and still do, my depression Has increased seven-fold over the past three months or so, causing me to say and do things I heartily regret, medication sickens me, to the extent I am physically ill just from putting a tablet into my mouth. I am sick, even before I attempt to swallow it. The thought of doing so, makes me sick to my stomach.

And it is true what they say. Medication can help some people with their depression, not everyone. It treats symptoms, is not a cure, and not for everyone. It is not for me. I know myself, my body, and its not. It just is not useful; to me to take these things. Why? I am so whacked out I don't notice my neighbour when he walks by and says hello. I feel so sick all the time. After six months, it is still the same. I feel worse, not in control of my own body. So I know it is not right for me personally. Since I have not taken it, I have come on in leaps and bounds. And I challenge anybody who says like wise. It helps the symptom. The depression is the symptom, and not the root problem. There are reasons for this, for depression.

Finding out what they are and utilising coping mechanisms is useful, I attempt to do so.
Now I don't know what they all are, and it seems to me that they must differ in each of us, since our experiences are all different, aren't they. Stop and describe is a good one, as is writing down my goals for the future, as is using the Buddhist principles of mindfulness.

But whatever your experiences, your feelings can make life so intolerable self harm, and suicide seems imminent, indeed the only option. I know this isn't true, as I have been, and still am, a self-harmer, and I have attempted suicide, and am still very suicidal much of the time, regardless of what others may think, say, and record in medical records. I know how I feel, but I am trying to balance that, with positives, people, things, looking at goals, dreams, and outrageous desires. I need to say that, first and foremost of these is to become a published, self employed writer, away from the retrace, and doing something nonstressful and of personal importance.

You never know, this book, my experience, could be my ticket to achieving that dream. This is positive, and because of this desire, I find now want to live, which is good. I want to join the ambulance service; I want to become a paramedic, as well as writing. There are so many places I want to see, so many things I wish to do. I have much to prove to myself.

All this is true, even though paradoxically I still often want to die. Strange how this can pervade my every day life isn't it? Even though things are going better for me now, I have a job, albeit voluntary, 16 hours a week, editing the magazine of the Leicester LGBT Centre. It is called large magazine. Not too original, but cool nonetheless. And the Centre has helped me as much as any other angency, they helped by accepting me for who I was, both sexuality, mental health issues, and everything. To them, I am just Adam, not a diagnosis, not an issue, or problem to be solved. Just a guy who hangs out and volunteers.

Things like this do help an awful lot it has to be said. But the suicidal urges are still there. I am trying to train myself out of that reflex. I just want to have a decent life, and achieve a few bits. I am not at all competitive, or ambitious, but I know there is more to life than this, and I can do more than I am. A life worth living, as that's all I ever wanted to begin with. As I have already stated, Medication can help some. It really is not for me, but maybe others, and support always definitely helps. Having people around who give a damn, not because they are paid to, but because it feels right to them, works wonders. Self esteem can only double in the face of affection. But it doesn't take away the pain you feel each day.

And when it does build, temptation looms, and it takes a real battle of will to ignore it. One day I believe, it won't be so tough. But that is in the future, and right now it certainly is. And do you want to know the terrible thing about all this? It is that even though I am beginning to regain hope, I am finding that depression and anxiety really stop me from wanting to eat, and this makes me feel weak, faint, end up in hospital, and get even lower. It is a vicious circle. And I know that's common. Knowing that I cannot allow this to continue any longer, to help myself, I have sat down, and actively tried to work out what I enjoy eating. (When I feel able to) and how I can use those food types to get myself to eat in a more healthy way.

To work this out I went back to my childhood and tried to remember what my favorite foods were then. Unsurprisingly, these have changed in the past few Years. Perhaps as I reached adulthood my palette has changed. I don't know, but I know I don't like chicken drummers and oxtail soup these days. In an attempt to get healthier, I have packed in all my old favorites (crisps, chocolate, burgers kebabs, crap basically) and I have discovered I like many cultures foods – but it has to be rustic, peasant food. And that is always filling; hearty you know what I mean? It is real working class food.

So, I of course love these old classics: broths, chowders, simple risottos, Tapas,
Anti-pasti, hotpots. And then, even better: simple stir-fry's, noodle and rice dishes, potato dishes, like mousaka, potato gratin. I like to think I am open minded, and will try anything once. I love Mexican food, refried beans, salsa, vegetables, and spices, all in tortias, burritos, enchiladas, and tacos, whatever. I also have a taste for open sandwiches, with ham,

olives, feta, leaves, and stuff like that. You can almost taste the health increase just by looking at it. I love a good, fresh and tasty soup, and that goes the same for a good tasty, interesting salad. I used to drink lots of Fizzy Drinks, but I don't so much now, though I still drink far too much coke. I have found that if I dissolve some sugar in a pan with some cherries, or strawberries, or fresh skinless apricots, it makes thick syrup. I filter this through a sieve, and when it's cold, I add sparkling water to it, mix it, and keep it for a day or so. It's lovely, natural, and very good for me. I also love smoothies, especially the "innocent" brand as it has no shit in it. Though I know that at times, I still drink far too much alcohol. I suppose this is foolish considering I have made all this effort thus far.

When I used to go out, I had Lager, or cider, but now I tend to relax at home more, I have discovered I much prefer wine, or ouzo to those. I am not much of a connoisseur when it comes to wine, all I know is, I like rose wine better then red, and white better than rose. That's all I know. I know red is supposed to go with certain stuff, and white with others, but I don't care. Give me a plate of Tapas, or pasta, a white wine, chilled music, and a book, and I am happy. End of story. Perhaps drinking at home isn't good, but it keeps the pain at bay.But that's by the by. Back to what I was talking about before, depression, the horrid feeling of impending doom, the suicidal tendencies that come with it – for me at least. I have this seriously bad tendency to drop back to rock bottom in seconds. Really have to pack it in.

It is really unhealthy, I find. I am so depressed it is unreal. But I have written a piece recently, that reminds me I have seen hope, and believe I can get better. That is still far off, but it is now inevitable I will survive and thrive, rather than not survive. So here it is, beyond the swirling mists of blue. I woke up in shadows, swirling blue mist, and choking fog surrounding me, I could not see, hear or breathe, I was lost alone, and a child again. Nothing made sense, nothing was real, just the keening wail of loneliness, which I was sure only I could here. Awareness bloomed; I found others within the mist, others who were victims of the darkness. We chatted, laughed, and played together, slowly the darkness lifted, the mists parted, and I was in a beautiful meadow, with sunlight beating down upon me. There was the fragrance of vanilla in the air, and birds flying above me, and the wind whistling in the trees.

The night had gone, the day had come, the depression had lifted, and I was free. I knew that I could go on, and find my place in the world. Sometimes, the mist settles heavy on the horizon, and I can barely see the meadow, but it matters not, because I know its there, and that's all that counts. I have seen a glimpse of hope, and I am holding onto that, ray of light.

I am not there yet, I am not yet recovered, but I am on the path, truly, this time, and can see it stretching into the valley, and up onto the mountain, where I will be delivered into a secure and healthy life. I was freed from the swirling mists and heavy shadows. These days, I keep my eyes on day to day events, but my mind, is always, on that meadow, and the sweet scent of vanilla. Recovery is possible; I have seen it, however briefly, in the meadow, beyond the swirling mists of blue. An old saying comes to mind right now: "Let's make like the Sheppard, and get the FLOCK outta here!" I like it so much; I think I will adopt it as my personal motto. That piece led to my thinking about how hard it is to see the positive sometimes, too. And that led to a slightly darker piece, although it too is hopeful. It's positive I feel, as it highlights the battle for survival. Here it is, then. "Choose life".

Choose Life

Choose Life'
Simple as that,
Isn't it?
Continue to Breath,

See Light of Day,
And feel the cool joy of life,
Like a gentle Breeze.

But when life is
Only a dull and bitter Concept,
Where you exist,
And only that –

When each breath,
Feels like a Thousand
Razor Blades,
Slipping down,
Down your torn throat?

When sight brings
Only the broiling storm clouds
Of your mind,
Its lightening bolts,
Searing your Soul,

And the breeze,
It strips away your essence,
Bit by bit,

Could you still?

Choose Life?
And would you want to.
That is the question,
Isn't it?

I'm not sure that I truly can,
Not Now,
Not Anymore.

You will have to forgive me, here; negativity drenched morderlin tendencies and a heavy sense of impending doom is upon me. And they are shadowing my thoughts. I think that piece holds a lot of pain for me. As I am going through a rough patch, as I am sure many others out there are too. So yes, I am strongly acquainted with pain, the physical, and the mental. And I hate it. And I want only for it to stop, to have some release from this endless torment. Recently I have had vivid flashbacks, like a video playing on the walls of my mind, which I cannot turn off, or mute. I can only rewind it, and fast-forward.

As I type this, the tape rewinds it self, only to play again, on constant repeat. Others have attempted to help me. Doctors, nurses, therapists and psychiatrists, all have really tried to help me. And so I have tried therapy, two different types, DBT and an inpatient therapeutic community, both of which did little for me. In small ways they helped yes, but not enough.

I felt therapy was far more judgemental, that the people who worked there felt their way was the only one, and if you didn't fully understand yourself you were wrong, and if you didn't like conflict you were hiding something. During my time in the first lot therapy I really struggled to deal with the attitudes. Here is a letter that I wrote to the consultant, and indicates in a clear way how I felt. So here it is:

104B Knighton Lane,
Aylestone Park,
Leicester,
Le28be

12 January 2004
Dr Campling
Francis Dixon Lodge,
Gypsy Lane,
Leicester
Dear Dr Campling,
Subject: my experiences of treatment at FDL

Dear Dr Campling,

I am writing to you regarding concerns that I have about the treatment I received, and the feelings I have about my time there, during both my admissions at Francis Dixon Lodge. On my first admission, I came to FDL vulnerable, and in a terrible state, Suicidal and unsure of where my life was heading. I saw this place, as a shot at a life, my only chance, and the culture there did nothing to alter this perception. Of course, now I understand the way FDL works' that we are meant to explore our differences, challenging our own behaviour, and that of each other.

I understand how this is meant to teach us about ourselves, and help us develop Citizenship, and understand ourselves whilst supporting us in learning how to deal with our interpersonal relationships in a better way, etc. It looked great, thought this was my one big chance to sort out my life, even though I realised it was not a cure.

In principle I agree entirely, that FDL has the potential to be of great help to people, and that the ideals behind it were quite groundbreaking. However as an ex-resident, I'm afraid to report that I did not quite find this to be the case. I came in at age 20, quite young in attitude, pretty immature, and unknowlegable. And I feel I was not properly prepared for the reality of FDL, I was not supported in any way by my sponsor of the time, but was too afraid and unsure of myself to make a complaint. I quickly came to fear the tempers of others and I buried myself. Now I do not blame anyone for my actions, but I do feel you should be aware of certain facts. . I'm sure that you will agree that being in FDL, is not easy, by any means, but are you aware of quite how tough it is?

As consultant you will not have experienced the bullying culture that seems to have appeared in recent years. It is no longer merely challenging, not nurturing in the least. On my first admission, I was bullied from the first, accused of attention seeking, made to feel less than manly, less than others. I was dictated to, my every move watched, my every reaction analysed. It was like being in prison!!

I have an issue with you and the community at that time, which I was never able to resolve successfully. I doubt you remember when the community tried to pin the thefts at that time on me back in 2000, although I no longer remember the month, or the exact date, it still plays on my mind. There was a series of thefts, from the common room, peoples rooms, etc and I was accused of these, because I was a loner, scared of the others, I sat alone, so I was blamed, but I wasn't guilty, and I was not believed, and my life was made a living hell for over a week, finally when I could not take the shouting and brow beating, harsh voices and the all consuming fear, I requested 7 days leave, intending to leave, I was so angry at the harshness, the unfairness of it all. I went home, and calmed down.

Over this period of time, my fear for my life, the suicidal urges came back in full force, the self-loathing, it all hit me. My abuse, everything haunted me, so I came back, apologised, even though I had a right to my anger! I was attacked, told how the 7 days leave made it look like I was guilty, that I had run away. I did not run, I needed space to clear my head, as well as having my own issues, I had to face the community making accusations, I was a scapegoat, I bore the brunt of others anger. I cow-towed, and internalised my feelings. From that moment all of my paranoia, feelings of non-acceptance, that I was hated despised, became real to me. I realise now I should have spoken up, took responsibility, but I was afraid, paralysed, afraid that those I needed to help me had abandoned me. So I lost faith in those who accused me.

I lost faith in the process, in the community, and in you, personally. You did nothing to ease the situation, at the time, it felt like you approved of what happened, I felt punished by you. Maybe this was wrong, but that was the way it felt at the time. Perhaps I didn't challenge it as I should've, but I feel let down, and I am hurt and angry over that. I no longer had the amount of trust necessary to do "the work" of FDL, just stopped talking about my issues, after all, every attempt to explain my feelings had always been shot down in the past, so I never got round to dealing with any issues there, and whilst I must take my own fair share of this, you are not entirely Blameless. Nor is the culture you allow to thrive.

Each day was a battle to survive, to not break down, and to fall under the heels of the community. One of my earliest issues with the way the culture was how I felt discriminated against because of my sexuality, I was bi-sexual, and was struggling to except that, but I wasn't listened to, was told to make up my mind, told I annoyed people by my uncertainty. I did not have the confidence in myself to argue back, and this destroyed my faith in myself for quite a while.

I find when I look back now, I see just how brainwashing the culture was, drumming it into our minds that the only way to be a "success" was to "leave properly" staying the course, doing your time, listening to "assessments" on your behaviour every 3 months? This is soul destroying, at least I found it so. What were we achieving? Doing what? I completed, came through to the end, had my "leaving do" joined next step did my year, and reached the cut of point. I did what was expected, and I really tried to live my life taking into account what I learnt at FDL. But it isn't possible! There was so much that I needed to tell the community, so much I needed to discuss, about the abuse I suffered, physical, emotional, and sexual, about my childhood, everything. But I didn't, because I couldn't. When you are put in a bullying environment, when that's all you have previously experienced, you cannot trust those who bully you. Experience teaches you better. How the hell are you meant to talk about deeply emotionally scarring experiences, when you fear the very people you are meant to talk too?

We cannot check out every issue with everyone, you cannot call a "crisis meeting in the middle of the night" FDL simply allowed the ones who were angrier and more confident to boss around those who were meeker and more afraid. It created a dictatorship, people were bullied, terrified of the few who were popular, those who gave the "feedback" feedback? It was pure malice half the time. And this was rarely challenged, in fact it was encouraged, conflict was fanned, deliberately b y the staff, I suppose it was meant to teach "citizenship" and "appropriate behaviour" these so call-challenging comments" drove people to tears, to self harm.

How does this help us with our issues? How? You told me nine months would be suitable when I first arrived, on my first admission, and so, I decided to leave at nine months, as the culture prevented me from progressing further, and I would only have slipped back further. So I quietly got trough my nine months, tried to do it right, tried to grow up, be mature, take responsibility, like a good little drone. Where did it get me/ I tried to support others until it came up to nine months, and left, and was relieved to be free! Free! Can you believe that?

I was so afraid, afraid of you that I was glad to leave. I thought if I stayed any longer I would break down, scream my anger, my pain, lose al control, and waste all my efforts thus far. I pretended to be ready, that it had worked, because I felt that was what was expected, it was part of the brainwashing. I put myself through all that. But I wasn't at all well, or ready. I needed more support then, at that point then I ever had before. I am angry with myself for leaving, for my fear, for everything. And I am angry with the culture for making me feel so helpless I needed to flee. It should have been a place of safety! But I left nonetheless, smiled my fake plastic smile, and endured hours of false humour and an atmosphere you couldn't breath it was that toxic. So I left, and I was told this was only beginning my journey. Oh, just how true that was.

I had come to realise I didn't handle my admission at all well, had regrets, things I needed to look at to deal with before I felt I could move on. I saw it was my responsibility to put right these issues, so I came into see Anthony brae, in outreach, to discuss my worries and concerns. It had reached the extent where I was having nightmares about FDL. We talked and decided my issues needed to be dealt with at the source. I agreed to come in for assessment, and was therefore admitted, 10th feb 2003, for the second time. My second admission was intended to allow me the space to deal with those issues that I have specific to FDL, and as such I looked forward to a productive if difficult, and long hard slog ahead of me. Alas, this was not to be the case. I was greeted with distrust and suspicion from the first. I assumed this to be paranoia, after all, it was my second admission, and how would the staff react to me? It turned out it wasn't the staff I should have worried about so much. The culture was the enemy. It had not changed at all. I was told that people found it hard to accept and deal with me, trust me, because I had come back a second time, and that the lodge had not worked for me. A lot of the residents felt FDL was their last chance, and I made it clear I had failed, therefore they had to face the thought it might not help them so much either.

If you're every effort to come back, face up to your responsibilities, your part in the troubles you have had, is blocked at every turn, what good is this?? You failed once, didn't make a go of it' you had this whole place, and still you are not better" this was a somewhat naive and distressing attitude. To be told "this is our one and only chance, we don't want to screw up like you did, you remind us it's possible, and you aren't welcome here" well, it makes you Angry. If the community will not accept you, allow you to reveal yourself and do the work, how can you do so? I had left gone through the leaving process, felt that pain, and yet here I was being lectured like a child "you don't understand it in here"

I was unable to do what I had to do, talk about my feelings regarding friends deaths, people I had known at FDL, talk about the theft incident, issues with my father, issues around rape and abuse etc. I could not do this in an environment where I was badly treated. This isn't ramblings of paranoia, a resident told me this, a resident who was still there after I left the second time, told me how people felt, the things they had been saying, and explained the air of mistrust around me. I would walk into a room, and all conversations would stop. I had felt this, and this person confirmed that. It was hardly conducive for therapeutic treatment. It seems to me these members of the community did not realise FDL wasn't a "cure" and were not taking personal responsibility. I was tormented by the past, and it felt repeated all over again, and I just couldn't stand the prospect of another 6 months or so at FDL in the same vain as my previous admission, I was so angry, disenchanted, that I left in an inappropriate way, I did not inform people, I jumped in a taxi, left behind stuff, because I was afraid of persecution, so I ran away. I'm ashamed I did that, and it cost me a lot of self-respect. But let me explain why. I left in that way, only because I felt it pointless. The community had already expressed their feelings about me. It seemed futile to go into a battle.

I wanted to give it a go, Dr Campling, Try again. See if it was I could do the work, see if I could make a go of it, I was trying to be responsible, and face up to my own shortcomings! The culture has stagnated to such an extent that the community instantly judged me, I feel, unfairly. The majority of the feedback I received was informal, out of meetings, so that the staffs were mostly unaware, I think, of the on goings. I should have spoken up, but it seemed so futile. So I take responsibility for the way I left, and apologise for that, if nothing else.

Let me explain how leaving feels. When people leave Francis Dixon Lodge' it is a horrendous time, a separation from an environment you can no longer easily live without. We are told this is because we form strong relationships, we form bonds not easily broken, we learn to trust and value each other. No it's because we become more institutionalised than we were before. This is my experience, and understanding of the process. I suffered hell, and after a month or so I was told I had left, not to seek support from staff on the helpline, this was appalling!! A month after nine months is nothing,

I feel hurt and angered, and my distress at this treatment pushed me back. I never brought this to next step, because I was so afraid of the culture. Even then, the fear I felt stopped me from conforming. I should have shouted, should have shown my pain, should have challenged this, but I did not. This is my responsibility, we are all individuals, and as such should stand up for ourselves, I understand this now, but that doesn't excuse FDL. This is not enough support'

So I put to you, that this is simply wrong. The cut off point is far too soon, too unstructured, it needs to be gradually brought it, slowly. So how can this be improved? I suggest that you send out questionnaires to all ex-residents, asking what support they would have proffered to have received on leaving and afterwards. Next step does not last long enough' although for most of us, I suspect it felt far too long, at the time! I also believe it would be beneficial if you was to offer ex-residents the come back and give feedback, air any outstanding issues they have around their time at FDL, because I believe you would be surprised at the result.

FDL in my opinion does not work, at all well, no as well as it could. But you never seem to get any negative feedback, it never seems to circulate, although I am aware it is a general; feeling amongst most ex-residents who have left for any amount of time, that it was hurtful, and did them more harm than good. But this is frustrating, because It could work far better, being a real success, if the processes involved were revised with the support of those who have experienced the service.
Please understand, I am not writing to attack the service, but to offer my opinion, and support, because

I truly believe in what FDL intends to achieve, and attempts to provide. Dr Campling, I think the way its run needs to evolve and change. Please take my comments on board. I still carry a lot of emotional baggage about my 2 admissions, and I am now starting treatment at woodlands soon, Thanks to Anthony and Dr Meakin, my psychiatrist. The best help I have received thus far is this referral, as I am now on the correct dosage of medication, and it seems I am finally about to get the help I need. And having discussed my feelings about FDL in my initial assessment at the woodlands unit, Friday 9th 2004-01 I feel I need to speak to you, lay my demons to rest, to be able to move on with my own personal recovery. To that end, I would very much like the opportunity to come and discuss my feelings around my treatment at Francis Dixon lodge and how it has affected my future.

I look forward to your response' and hope that you have not found this letter to upsetting or incendiary. It has not been meant as a rant, or an angry tirade, but as an effort to speak about my feelings. To recap, I would very much like to discuss this matter further with you. Thank you for your time, and I hope this hasn't been too much of an inconvenience to you,

Yours sincerely,

Adam Pick

So as you can see here, every day was a torment. In the second lot of therapy, I found a stiff unbending attitude in my therapist, she misunderstood my concern about a lump on my thigh near my testicles, thought I had said I had cancer, when in actual fact I had said I was anxious about whatever it was.

It got back to my doctor who thought I had lied about her diagnosis, it all got out of control, and it took a long time to clear up. All because the therapist was hasty, judgemental, bossy, and did not listen. She overheard someone talking about me second hand and leapt into action, shouted at me in our one to ones, and she aced inappropriately. And I handled her attitude inappropriately too, which I apologised for. But therapy has not been of much use to me really. That's not to say I have always said and done the right things. I have at times been a royal pain, but too often people judge others without trying to understand, and I feel I have had this experience.

I have had three admissions to an acute ward within hospital, several admissions to the crisis resolution team, and there has been little improvement in my mood, in fact, there has been none. This made me realise that I was looking in the wrong direction, for too long I saw my issues as a matter of mental illness, but now I realise this is not so. It is a spiritual one, drained by the world I live in, and the pain I have suffered I had given up. I had given up on a spiritual level. This drove me to look into Buddhism for five years, Confucianism and Taoism came next, followed by three years with the Jehovah's witnesses. Even though all the people I met during this spiritual search were lovely, it was not for me. Then in late 2005, it hit me. I wanted to find god.

Why didn't I try a church? I know this sounds obvious. But the person who abused me had gone to church, and this marked the church as a dangerous place to be. I was a child. Some lessons are hard to undo. But undo it I did, and I found an Anglican church full of lovely people, and so I became a Christian at holy trinity church in Leicester. My pain has not gone, but god helps me to deal with it, and I have a purpose again. This purpose is to try and help others. And follow Christ's example as best as I can. Not an easy task, I grant you.

I have been lucky enough in the past, to have a friend, a shoulder to cry into, someone to hug and hold me tight, and that helped, but the time past, onward into memory, and I have that comfort no more. Nothing helps, what can? My mind hates me, of that I am reasonably sure, my subconscious minds, conspiring to destroy the conscious. Isn't that a strange thought? It is trying to reduce me to the state of a gibbering vegetable; why else would it heap upon me memory, after memory, scar, after scar?

And so the panic, the raw fear wells up in me now. It rises up only to join the pain that beats in me like a second heart. And then it happens: the anger comes up to meet them, to join, to merge, into one irrational whole, failingly. There will be no sleep for me tonight, then. As indeed, there has been none for the past two nights. Is this to be my fate? A living vessel, fit only to hold the negative, without ever being able to taste, the ambrosia, that nectar, which comes from being one with the positive?

Logically, I know this is not, cannot, be the case, although I am not really feeling that logical at this moment in time. Please do not see this as wholly negative, for I do not. Obviously, it isn't exactly positive either, but I do know enough by now, (I was a very slow learner though) to realise, that in the end, life isn't positive or negative. its not a bed of roses, or a terrible thing. Of course it is not. It is never wholly either, merely a combination of the two.

So I will have my day in the light, At least this has been my experience thus far. It is true, I am only 26, but this doesn't make me inexperienced. Please try and be opening minded. I have lived, experienced, and seen much. I can only hope that the things I see and experience, in future, are at least, a little more positive! At this point, I realise that my suicidal attempts were never going to help. Back then I wanted to die, I truly did. I was aiming only at ending the pain. And that is quite an insight for me. It may sound silly to you, but not for me. The overdoses, the attempted drowning etc, all of the suicide attempts and self harm. These were merely early and imperfect attempts at escaping the pain. I foolishly thought I would be achieving something spiritual by death.

 Becoming one with my destiny, and I guess it's the destiny for all sentient and living beings, to make these mistakes, during their existence. I intend to leave these behind me now, as I try to make my way into the future. I have baggage, as I will continue to have, but I don't want to live that way any longer, suicide attempt, after suicide attempt, cut after cut. Waking up in the morning wondering how to end it, and whether or not I feel bad enough to call the CRT…

This is not the life I want, the way I want my life to be. And so it is time to take a hold, get a grip somehow. I intend to write myself out of this, be my own therapy, my own counsellor, I intend to go back to work; I intend to live a full life. Not symptom free, perhaps, I am not that naive, but it will no longer dominate me. I intend to start living, truly, living.

There is yet another poem that I have written, which to me at least, tells my story. I was trying to fight the depression. That seemed endless, holding onto "I" working at going from pain to desperation. Going through some very bad experiences, meeting workers, people who I thought would complete me. Learning otherwise was a hard lesson. I went through so many forms of self harm attempting to gain a sense of myself, since the nine months I spent in FDL I have put on so much weight.

This was due to compulsive eating whilst in the community I was referred to. I didn't eat a lot of their food, because I felt judged, as if I was being watched constantly, and I hated to eat around them as we had to. It was meant to encourage a sense of community in us, but it merely encouraged my paranoia. And so I found ways around it. I went to the shop every night, and snuck food, chips, burgers and kebabs into my room, and used an air freshener to get rid of the evidence in case someone came in. that was six years ago. I am now well over 13 stone. I am not exactly fat, but carrying a few extra pounds, and according to my body mass index, I am obese for my height. When I am at my worst I cannot stop eating, I shovel it in, meal after meal, eating until I can feel it sitting heavily in my stomach.

I then go into the bathroom, close my eyes and will myself to retch it up. I have that strangest of abilities… I can make myself sick at will. It a reflex, you just have to search for it, and it happens. These days I eat only once a day, as a kind of mental control, it's not a punishment exactly, more of a reminder of how I can get to be, and my reluctance to keep living that way.

I do not think of myself as a bulimic, haven't done since 2000, where I used to make myself sick in the therapeutic community I was in, but I have had periods where I have binge eaten and threw up, most recently a month or so ago, where I did it for almost a week. For me it is a form of self harm, a way of dealing with emotions and stuff. At the moment I am attempting to get rid of the weight, so I can rid myself of the last reminders of this time. I have attempted to drown myself, took two overdoes, cut myself, carved into my arm, stuck darts in my arm as deep as I could, which just caused a small dot scar… I have used drink and even psychiatric drugs as self harm, taking so many I felt so, so ill… which is why I cannot take it any longer without retching uncontrollably.

I have used exercise and even work as self harm, pushing myself so hard, to prove I am good, am worthwhile… there has been so may different ways I have self harmed, and for so many different reasons as well. As a reward for getting through a bad day, as a reward for doing well, as a punishment if I feel I have hurt someone, or if I feel ashamed or guilty. I used to harm everyday a few years ago, for a different reason almost every time. I have my reasons for self harming others and have their own, and I have come to realize self harming is an intensely individual thing, not only changing from person to person, but different reasons sometimes, why men and women harm. Though this can be the case, I have found most often we respond to the same stimuli, and men are just as disturbed by events as women, just as unable to cope, but stigma gets in the way…. And Self harm is 99% of the time not attention seeking. That is something that really gets up my nose. The notion that people are inappropriately attention seeking. I am not denying it occasionally happens, but tarring everyone with that brush is simply not acceptable or useful. We need a culture change in regards to this I feel.

Things are changing, but slowly. It is changing a little too slowly for my liking. More on all this a bit later, but firstly I want to chat a little about self harm, generally. So. Let's talk about self-harm. Quite a pretty term isn't it? It is used to describe something that isn't too pretty, at all. I sincerely hope by the end of this session you will feel that you personally, have a general idea of the subject, the how's, whys, and wherefores of the whole business including what constitutes self-harm in the literal sense' and more importantly enabling you to develop a broader Sense of some of the reasons behind this disturbing phenomena. And it is disturbing; both for us, who do it, and for those who have to cope with us doing such things, such as loved ones.

And so, today you will hear from the real experts, from the actual self-harmers themselves, including myself. There is only certain extents of understanding that can be reached unless you have experienced the phenomena of self harm yourself, but I hope to assist you a little in gaining that understanding.

I hope that by listening to me ramble on like a right old moaner, you become aware of the support we all need from each other, and the things that you can easily do or say, that can make such things worse, such as condescending, and looking down on people struggling, or treating them as idiots. I don't claim YOU will do this, but people do sometimes, this has certainly been experience, and it made ME far worse.

So what IS this thing we call SELF-HARM?

> "Self-harm is the physical causing of deliberate harm to ones own body in order to deal with overwhelming feelings."

> And it is neither something to feel ashamed or guilty about. I seriously want you to listen to this. And listen well, please. It is NOTHING to be ashamed of. It takes a long time to come to term with that, at least it did for me. It is however, extremely unimportant how often people self-harm. That is, it could be once a month, or once a week, several times a day, or somewhere in between. It doesn't matter at all. I don't care a fig about how often, that isn't the issue. People who think it is are looking in the wrong direction.

> The things that are important is how badly one harms, whether or not the injury needs medical attention or not, and the reasons why one feels the need to harm. Sometimes it can feel you have no choice, and it's the reasons behind that, that are truly important. Now, there are many, many reasons why somebody turns to self-harm. It can be abuse, mental, physical, or sexual, but this isn't necessarily the case. Everybody is different, and so are his or her triggers. Understanding this is a

key element to helping the harmer. It is crucial. Self-harm is quite simply a coping mechanism and it can be positive or negative. It can be a positive act, a cut off valve that stops the feelings from reaching such a high pitch where you feel the only option is suicide.

At least, that's how self-harm served ME. So, if we are able to understand that it can allow a person to cope with a bad space in there lives ,where they are tempted to turn to less healthy methods of dealing with their feelings, such as alcohol or substance abuse, or possibly allowing there feelings to escalate to the point where suicide seems the only appropriate response. Please remember that this does not make them freaks or crazy, nutters or any other type of strange. They are peopling like you or I. We all do things we know are not good for us. The self-harmer merely takes it a step further. Consider: Some people smoke. Some drink. Some over do the fast food. Some do all three. These are all forms of self-harming. It's just that some are more socially acceptable than others.

I feel it would be beneficial for us to look at the different types of self harming, not all of them (as we don't have the time, and nobody can tell you all of them – there are new and interesting ways to harm the body that are being found every day). But let's look at some of the more common place ones.We have already mentioned eating too much, drinking and abusing substances excessively, but here are two very common ways that people use a lot: -

Overdosing – this counts for some 80% percent of self-harmers' statistically, followed by cutting which is the next most favoured method of self-harming. But let's look at some others, as well: -

Starving oneself-

Picking of scabs and scars
Burning of the flesh
Hitting oneself, either with fists or an object
Getting into fights
Tattooing or piercing (there are people who have many to hurt themselves; they get off on the pain.

Banging of the head
The deliberate breaking of bones
The deliberate doing of activities that could easily result in you being seriously injured.

These methods are generally none lethal, compared to some of the more extreme forms of self-harm. These are not as common, as indeed, they can only be done once. But in some cases, the mutilation of eyes, or self-castration, or the deliberate removal of limbs, do happen. This is a both very disturbing, and a mind numbing reality. The thought of it makes me sick, personally. I have felt so bad I wanted to slash my wrists, but feeling you have to be that extreme? It scares me. And I hope it scares you too. Because that is some peoples only reality. There then, were some very different ways of self-harming. Now the reasons why somebody does resort to self harming is a lot more difficult to comprehend –

The reasons are often very personal and indeed, very complex. I am a harmer, and so can suggest some reasons why people MAY self-harm, but I can only go on my experiences. I can give you no definite reasons why OTHERS will harm. People vary greatly remember. That is why self-harming comes in so many forms.

But here are a few common reasons why people may, and do harm.

- Relief from psychological pain
- Release of mounting tension
- Inability to feel
- Or feeling too much
- Inability to handle anything, either good, or bad
- Wanting to feel something, anything,
- Expressing an inner rage that you cannot explain
- Self harm can also be a celebration – it can help to feel alive, and grounded.
- Attention – not often the case, but it can be. I have used it in this way, albeit very rarely

Now, let me make this a little more personal. For me, self-harm isn't about a cry for help though, or even a cry of attention. It long since moved beyond those reasons. No, now it is only a cry of pain. When I am no longer able to verbalise how I feel, or logically work it through, in the recesses of my brain, I result to cutting. I can see the blood, flowing redly, and it shocks my brain back in to some semblance of order. Then the endorphins are released, with the adrenalin, and I feel like a god. For a while, I feel great, on top of the world.

Now I want to talk about the statistics of self harm, regarding the split, or difference between the ratios of self harming, regarding the two sexes. Statistically it seems that women more regularly self harm then men. The main reason for this they say, is that men ore far more likely to take it out on others, more likely to display, there hurt, pain and aggression whatever, by being violent and aggressive to others. Perhaps in the past, this was true, but no longer. It's a sexist attitude to assume this is always the case. Men can act in, this way true, but not always, and not exclusively.

There are many women who act in this way too. It's a myth, misconception, and stigma. In fact the rate of male self-harmers is nearly that of the female self-harmer. But because women are statistically more likely to go and get hep for various psychological problems including self injury, clinicians tend to treat more females than males. Why is this, what causes this? Well, this may be because men feel intimidated by the fact that a the literature out there is pretty much geared for women, or hey, maybe its that when a guy has a bunch of cuts and scrapes, or real bad bruises, they assume it's the signs of a rough sports fanatic, footie, rugby, martial arts, whatever. Or they assume he was just being a "real bloke" getting into a fight or three, after one to many beers.

Whereas with girls, this so obviously just isn't the case. It usually isn't assumed or seen to be the signs of a rough sports fanatic. No. Rather the girl is questioned about the source, and is less apt to be believed if she claims it to be a "blading" accident or something similar.

What I am trying to point out is the medical profession are far more likely to force her into some kind of treatment for her self-inflicted wounds, and her mental state. This is why, in my opinion, it is more women appear to be treated than men. This is wrong. It is sexist, bad for both the men, and the women. So why is it we have this pre-conceived idea that men won't hurt themselves? We need to get with the programme, people. We need a far more balanced view if all people are to get the hep they need. Minds need to be touched. Men don't always get a lot of compassion, but we're not all hard, or tough, some of us actually hurt very easily. That is the height of ignorance and these views need to be changed. They MUST be CHALLENGED!

It is generally assumed that Women, on the other hand, tend to turn that hurt and pain inwardly, on themselves. This is no more or less the case than men. So these stereotypes are harmful – they prevent true understanding of any of the issues involved. There is still much misunderstanding, and we really need to try and prevent this. Just thinking about injustices men and women go through, regardless of culture religion colour or creed always makes my skin blister and my blood boil, figuratively speaking. It also brings up much from my past, my own self harming urges, and memories of friends who couldn't cope and ended their lives, so tragically. It is hard to cope with, day in and day out and it's very hard at times to squish it all back down.

As im sure you can appreciate, this is not a period of my life I like to revisit, this book is extremely hard for me to write at times, as I can feel what I felt then… like its all playing on a cinema screen, and my eyelids are the screen itself. But I did eventually manage to get a slight sense of myself, my morals scruples, beliefs etc, more of which I will explore with you later, but I have a fledgling sense of "Adam" and I knew that this was the start of my recover, and so I had to start to discover myself more fully. I really had to search deep .I still am doing .Learning about who I am.

Doing this by exploring goals, dreams, desires, through research, and writing this book. This is of course my chosen method of finding out whom I truly am. It is the whole purpose of this book. No, that is not true. It started that way. But now I want to help others if I can, by sharing my experiences. Perhaps others will identify some with my semi literate ramblings. In this way, I hope to regain the friends I have lost along the way. They were good, true, and kind. Very cool people. That is a great source of sadness to me. I did people harm whilst I was ill, whilst I was psychotic, hurt some very wonderful people. And it is my profound hope that by writing this book I can reach out, and mend some of the broken fences in my life. I can make amends and gain back their trust. The next poem resounds heavily with these themes. So here it is, ""here, I sit, crying"

Here I sit, crying...

Here I sit, crying.
I cry, because I am all-alone now.
But I remember how it felt,
To be loved,
 Oh yes.

How I remember. Remember the ghosts,
Of the friends, and the family,
Those who were mine,
And I thought they would be –
Mine forever.

But they've all gone now.
So I sit here,
Crying. I am alone now, once again,
 I am Alone.
Why? And For what?
WHY?

Because I am gay.
A queer, a poof.
A beast –
Freak of nature,
Unnatural.

I still remember.
Yes, oh yes,
I cannot forget the taunting,
The beatings…
And the rape.

Here I sit crying.
I'm all-alone now,
But I remember,
 I remember how it felt,

To be loved,
Oh yes.

I remember the family'
The friends,
 or those who pretended to be
such.
But they are just that,
A memory,
A shade,
A glimpse of what could've, should've been,
But wasn't.

I miss them.

But in losing them I gained something worth,
A whole lot more,

MYSELF.

That hurts, to read that. It reminds me of the wrong I have done in my life, and makes me desire repentance all the more. I have prayed for forgiveness, and I know it has been given, but I still feel tainted. My mind is beginning to twist now, folding in on itself, merging with itself, becoming something strange and alien. I think I need to stop, and rest. Sleep would help, as I am exhausted mentally, yet, ironically I spend very little of my time asleep. And this kills me, as insomnia is a terrible thing, a sound rending, and spirit depriving experience.

Sitting here still, as the hours are passing, I watch the world fade from the colours of day, to a deep dark endless blue. Fading then to a dull and listless brown, that seems lit up by the lights below it. And then finally to black, the jet black of night as this city closes on down. Twilight has long since been and gone, the noises of the day replaced by the quiet shifting ones of the night, The rusting of the wind in the trees outside is the only accompliment to my typing. I sit here, sipping lemon tea (my latest attempt at getting off of caffeine and attempting to become one with the world of hot drinks) and watching my cat as she lies there, watching me. She is wonderful. Her name is beautiful. And she is that. She is a true companion. She is ever present, as she doesn't sleep so well, either.

Sleep doesn't come easily to the guilty, or those in pain. I guess I am lucky, as my pain is entirely internal, a product of the mind. I have no physical condition, so I am lucky I suppose. If you can call mind numbing, muscle racking terror lucky.

The pubs are long since closed, and the dancers and revellers long since departed the shiny clubs, and pool-halls. Nobody passes by under my window now, just the occasional stray dog, or the odd crisp packet. There are no lights on, in the houses across the street. I count 11 of them, and there are no lights there, none. So the people are in the land of nod. And I envy them. They really are lucky folk. And they really are. Sleep would be good… Yes, oh god let me sleep.

Now the wind has stopped, so nothing moves. It feels like I am the only human awake now, although I know that cannot be the case. As the night turns to day in other climes, in other parts of the world, as the living there start their day, and I am awake, up with them as I sit here typing. I am always Typing. Here I am always with the bloody typing. Sleep. Such a pretty word is sleep. It is lovely. It really is a glistening and untarnished jewel of a thought. It entices me, teases me, with small glimpses, caressing me like a lover, and then cruelly snatching its tender embrace away, jilting me, like only a lover can.

It's been so long now since it came to me easily. Now it has to be forced, induced by the chemicals swirling around my bloodstream, slowly trying to pull me under, drag me into the darkness. But to no avail. Because it seems that my mind will not give in. I will not conform. No I have too many thoughts to think, it seems. I have a lot to remember and to recall. No sleep for this boy, one more night to add to my mental list, as the world turns. It always keeps on turning.

I have this condition, its called insomnia. I think that is its name. I wonder what it means, actually. I know what it means to me: nightmare, an endless, tormented lack of rest, as my soul twists and turns, as my mind turns to mud, and my sanity departs me. My pain has come to life now, and my memories are real. They parade on the insides of my eyelids, never ending, laughing as they go. Stop this damn you. Stop. Please. Must I beg? Surrender my last scrap of dignity? My own mind hates me. Of this I am reasonably certain, and sure. Why would it insist on doing this, if it did not?

The voices from the past come back to me, in Dolby digital sound. They are amplified, so loud my eardrums threaten to blow. But only I can hear them. This is fucking awful, and I fear I can stand it no more. The pain has increased, first a dull ache, like the one that places you in the dentist's chair, then the throbbing, like the beating of a heart. I am in pain. It is the mind rending pain of a snapped and broken bone. Oh god, let me sleep.

My clock glows dully, as I watch the hands ticking, luminously, in the dark. Homer Simpson seems to be mocking me, as he stares out of the clock. He is a truly hateful character. I am going to bin him later, I swear I am. It's Half four am now. And in another hour, the world will begin to move quicker now, as people wake, and get ready to depart for work, the late shift-workers replaced by those in the day. Six am to six am. I remember those, the 12-hour shifts. Better than sitting here, without cause, and without purpose. I wish I still had the endurance to do those, it was hard yes, but no harder than living, and the pride I felt, ah. The pride I felt.

This is a feeling I have not felt in some time, now. And do you know what tortures me, the thing that rips and rends my soul? I have nobody to hold, and so no comfort is to be mine, and I know of none. Oh please, someone save me from this, I cannot do this, not again. Another twenty-four hours of the hustle and bustle of life, only to be replaced by the loneliness of the night once more. And so this is my punishment, or so it seems, to be awake, forever awake now. I see on the cinema screen of my mind, a new flick, one of my childhoods past, and it is mine. Oh god, let me sleep.

 Are others sitting staring at flickering screens, laying down, watching the walls? Do others share in my private torment, stalked by their own private demons? They must be I am sure. For they never leave me alone. They are always there. They are my silent and loyal companions in the dark. I think that I may start taking drugs, of the illegal kind I mean. Probably beats the psychiatric ones I used to take. No I won't. Not really. It is a tempting thought though. Cannabis, now there's a thought. Maybe that's the way sleep will finally surrender herself to me, coming on strong, like a friend, like a loved one.

And I would love her forever, as she enfolded me, in her dark, dark embrace. But she is a bitter and jealous mistress, and I cannot trust in her charms, for she mocks me, and I fear she always will. Oh fuck, that's it, I am losing it finally, and I can feel my mind, as it trickles down my back, turning to sludge. God, I love you, I follow you with an open mind and with love in my heart, but won't you give me some relief? Or are my sins that bad? Please, give me sleep.

Oh god. Let me sleep, please, let me sleep. Well, that's very unlikely to happen, considering god seems to hate and despise me. and if not, I can more than make up for that, all by myself, though, I expect, many people who have passed through my life would feel the same. friends have come, stuck around a bit, and then gone, those who gave me there friendship, best friends, in some cases, then grew tired of me, and left. I am sure they hold a little hate, or dislike for me, and this in itself, this knowledge serves only to keep me awake, and sink me into further depressions.

So if I am to stay awake then at least let me speak of something that has in the past bought me immense pleasure. Of what do I speak? Books dear reader, books. I love them, I love the fact that the author creates a whole world for you to devour every chill, every thrill, is plotted, and calculated to produce an emotion. I have many favourite books, but I feel it may be more telling to share my favourite Authors instead, as fellow lovers of books will be able to tell a little about me maybe, by my selection.

Favorite authors

Arthur C Clarke, Phillip K dick, The Dalai Llama, Diane Weekes, Ray Bradbury, William Gibson, Douglas Adams, Eric LustBader, David zindell, J.R.R Tolkien, Jack London, Mark Twain, George Orwell, Roald Dhael, Philip Jose Farmer, William Burroughs, Thich Nhat Hanh, (very cool author of Buddhist principles), Wayland Drew, Cooper, William Goldman, John VornHolt, Neal Gaiman, Kafka (I am a recent convert to both of these – I spend a lot of my spare time in the library right now) Douglas Hill (wrote some excellent teen-fiction, which is now out of print, mostly), Ursula Le Guin,

J.K.Rowling (sad I know, but I admire her ability to write on different levels.. that's my story and I am sticking to it!), Michael Moore, Frank Herbert, L. Ron Hubbard, Franklin W. Dixon, and far too many others to document here! (What can I say, I am a bookworm.) I love books, very much so. But my love of books does not end with the modern.

I have a deep love for old and antiquated books, books that have a musty smell to them, yellowing pages, aged and fragile. It's funny, the older the book, the more I enjoy reading it, as if I am inheriting shared wisdom, that is flowing up and through me, as the years roll back, and the knowledge of those that went before me. Life was harder then, poverty was snapping, and biting, clawing at their ankles… cars were primitive, the price of living was less, and yet more at the same time, speech and clothing were old and strange, to us, at least.

I often sit and wonder, if these old authors, from the early 1900s were taken from their time period, and dropped into our own/ what would they make of aeroplanes, trains, trams, videos, DVD's, computers, the fashions of today, the way we speak and everything… the cultures we have, all mixed together in our cities, like a huge melting pot. To us, this is normal, to them, It must surely seem magical, weird, confusing, and very frightening. I would imagine. Trying to explain modern concepts to a 1900's gentleman would be most interesting, and I love to imagine how it would go. Would they cope, or would their minds snap, unravelling, unwinding, only to lie in an unwieldy heap on the floor.

And music, writing, literature, and Art… Cubism, and Picasso, surely they would think it insane? They would surely find us indecent savages, our mannerisms, our swearing, our way of dealing with our everyday lives. Then, gentlemen were gentlemen, with strict ways of acting, speaking, communicating with our fellows, but now… we are a lot more relaxed, laid back, informal…

The thought amuses me very deeply… it makes me laugh, until I believe my sides would split. But what if, we were plucked from our era, and flung back through the mists of time to find our selves in the late 1800's… it would be hideous, we would be lost, our frame of reference would be inadequate to deal with the reality of life at that time in history. The thought chills me to the bone… truly a nightmare experience. Though, I am sure there are those, for whom a slower, older, more measured, and formal way of life, would be beneficial, perhaps to be preferred. More decent, more civilised, more exquisite…but not tome. No, to me, it's an arty-farty period of time, blow hardy, and false….

It seems it was all about concealing emotion, etiquette, broken hearts and screaming minds being hidden behind a smile and a cheery wave. It seems soulless, maybe the origin of the British stiff upper lip. It is all horrendous, at least in this era we are much more honest. Its true life is tough, crime is on the rise, wars are rife, but we don't hide emotion as much… perhaps that's the key. It could be the starting point for all nations to talk to each other for once. I don't know. So getting back to my original thought; the early 1900's would be desirable to some…

A golden era. I find myself wishing that I lived in any time, space, era, that wasn't this one, in a vain hope that I could somehow be magically transmogrified in to a happy being. That by living in a different space than the one I currently find myself in, things would be different. I have fantasized that I was born in Japan, during the era of the samurai. Where bushido was king and honour was everything. I wish that I had been born Greek. I wish I had been born around the time of Plato or Aristotle. And that I had been a philosopher. This is true in that living in the country is healthier than in the city, simpler, less stressful. Environment plays an important part in human development, but so does internal factors, such as desires, personality, and sense of truth. It's all interlinked somehow…

But in my wiser moments, I realise it's not the physical space, so much as the mental space you inhabit. Moving, living in a slower environment, could help, yes, indeed, but the true change, must come from within, and that, alas, is not so easy. A change of heart, mind, soul, comes slowly, and at a price. The growing pains are painful, indeed. But it will happen, I will grow, I will shed the old skin, much like a snake in the grass, my ethics will change, merge and I will be a new being. As a new Christian, I truly believe my life will change for the better, as I develop my personal relationship with god, and learn to live my life according to the example set down by Jesus, when he died on the cross so that I may live, and stand before god in the new system of things.

So whilst I struggle, I know now that I am protected, and will not commit suicide no matter how bad life becomes for me. As long as I have a mustard seed of faith, that is not an option for me. So growth will happen. Life will move on and I will get there. I will, by pure will power alone, if that becomes necessary. But it won't ever come to that, because I believe in god, and know he will get me through as long as I believe in Jesus and live me life in his name.

Knowing I have God in my life, I know I am different to the beginnings of human life, in that I know I have a creator; they didn't have knowledge, but mere instinct. Thinking on this, I wonder if the social isolation we all feel, in the depths of the soul, the misery, the loneliness, the need for the pack animal within each of us, to be with its fellows, has this lessened or worsened, over the ages? Will our venerable ancestors relate to us on the emotional level, or will be as strangers, separated by a boiling, sea of time? As I am separated from my ancestors by knowledge and awareness, I feel I am separated from my fellows by mental attitude, by my perception of the world around me, or lack of perception. Perhaps that is more accurate.

There is a favourite pieces of prose of mine, which seems to add up quite nicely, the end of a sum, the final calculation, an understanding of the different and strange, and how its usually not so strange, the mad not so mad, the crazy not so crazy, If seen in context, if all the facts are known, than madness, becomes mundane, and old hat. But if you couch it in individual perception, add description, it becomes much more vital, throbbing with life. Yes, it becomes alive.

This piece by Emily Dickenson gives me much hope:

'Much Madness is divinest Sense'

**Much Madness is divinest Sense –
To a discerning eye –
Much Sense – the starkest Madness –
'Tis the Majority
In this, as All, Prevail –
Assent – and you are sane –
Demur – You're straightaway dangerous –
And handled with a Chain –**

EMILY DICKINSON (1830 -86)

I find myself bolstered by this poem, strengthened, Knowing, if you differ from the moral majority, you risk being labelled, and cast out of Eden, The recognising, that being a little odd, strange, is the most logical thing, when the world around us is deranged, and crazy, off its little head. Terror is a powerful motivator, and in these days of bombings, attacks, and suchlike, is it not practical to become a little unhinged? We are a product of our society after all?

We do have free will, but there are factors in our environments which pre-dispose us to certain actions. Madness, I feel, is one of them. But of course, now I have taken refuge in god, I recognise him as mighty, holy, and wonderful, my god, my heavenly father; this is no longer as true. I need not seek shelter deep in my own mind, cut off from reality, but seek it in his word. This may be a big factor in my recovery. The human world makes no sense, but Gods word is full of sanctuary for me.

But I still find myself slipping back into psychosis at times. Feeling I am immortal, energy, that cannot be destroyed or created, I just am, and have always been, without thought or volition. That when I die I will just go back to energy. This may be the case, as god created all… I don't know. But I was absolutely convinced that it didn't matter if I killed myself as my essence would exist forever. Happily, I no longer hold this view. At least this is not the case whilst I am well.

All of a sudden, as I sit here writing, the sensible side of me grows distant, fades into black darkness, and the wild, unkempt strong bit of me rears on u and shatters my new found calm. I find that my mind is turning backwards, inwards on itself, twisting and turning, looping in circle, so that I am back in my past, re-living the things I have lived through once, and survived barely. I did not ask for this return journey, and do not welcome, or relish where it is taking me.

 Childhood, and the Child, period, is beautiful, or at least it should be, a time of innocence, and a time of immense possibility and wonder it should be shiny, like the sun, but alas this was not the case, for me, or many others .It was a time of fear, of shadows and demons It was a time of uncertainty when I should have had reassurance. This poem, by Silvia Plath, adds it up, shows me what life could have been like. that in a mirror world, an alternate dimension, where, dark is light, trauma, pleasure, and the things that go bump in the night, dare not show there faces. Where life is only what it seems, and there is not a heavy feeling to the atmosphere, no fear, no terror.

"Child"

Your clear eye is the one absolutely beautiful thing.
I want to fill it with colour and ducks,
The zoo of the new

Whose names you meditate –
April snowdrop, Indian pipe,
Little

Stalk without wrinkle,
Pool in which images
Should be grand and classical

Not with this troublous
Wringing of hands, this dark
Ceiling without a star

SYLVIA PLATH (1932 – 63)

Thinking back to that time, my heart jumps up into my mouth, and I can feel the tears coursing down my face. Memories of sexual and mental abuse rush into my mind, and are quickly met with the knowledge my own father attempted to strangle me to death. Dear God, the pain is too much. Maybe I should not have started this path so soon, the poems I read, the places I have been, only serve to turn me deeper inside, and to show me pieces of myself I am perhaps not ready to see. The dark places within me. But I shall not turn aside, or look away. This is my therapy, my voyage of self discovery, and I shall persevere… it is a way of healing I believe, because we all have the capacity to heal ourselves, through God's grace.

Knowing this strengthens my resolve, but does little to stem the tide. And so, memories are coming thick and fast now, totally unbidden, and unwanted, flashbacks to a time and a place where I was in danger, both physical and mental, a time where I was not my own master.

I was not my own master, but subject to the whims and desires of those who were meant to be my mentors, protectors, guides in a world which seemed to hate me. But I received no guidance, only abuse. This came in two forms both mental and physical. What was really the beginning of the corruption of my soul? As a child I was pure and complete. But the heart and soul of a young boy, who knew nothing, and wanted to know everything was torn asunder… I was an innocent, an empty canvas, on which anything could be painted, arts of great beauty. But this was not to be the case. the pictures on my canvas, which last through till today, were ones of brutality, and pain, inked in blood and tears, sweat and excrement.

Let me now, show you a little of my past, my childhood, the events that conspired to make, me… well, me, I guess. I have already mentioned physical sexual and mental abuse, but you need to understand the contest of all that, how it all happened, as well as what actually happened, to get a sense of how it made me, the person I am. I know I am responsible for how I act ultimately, but as I have already said, environmental factors are of huge importance to a developing sense of self.

As a child, I learned to create my own "Reality" a space that was at the same time, both imagination, and the place I lived, dwelled in. it was a phantom region, far distanced from that of my fellows. As I milled about, automaton like, as a child, it was the only friend I really had. A place of super-villains and heroes, where good always won out, the evil in people was always punished, and pain, was easily wiped away. It was a place of innocence.

This place in my head was brought about mainly due to inability to relate to others my own age at first. My issues began in primary school, but I survived this quite well. The next step was to be much more problematic for the young Adam. Secondary School was just another threat, one of many, danger lurking in the hallways of this harsh and cruel institution. It was awful. A scary place, mocking me with its "lessons" although the hardest of all, that I was forced to learn, were not the ones on any official agenda.

"Don't walk full corridors, for they will see you. And that will be bad – you get hurt when they see you"
"Do not be seen, at all, by your peers, above all, do not be heard"

Going to and for Dinner was a no-no, too scary and dangerous. I did manage it some days, but others, I would hide in the toilets near the music rooms, as that part of school was nearly always quite at lunch, and force myself to be sick, vomiting away the fear, the pressure, until I became calm. But they would see me, they would hear me, and so the beatings would come. And they would utter meaningless words to me, strange and sibilant, chatter that might as well, have been in Martian, for all the sense it made to me.

It did not seem real. That is unlike my own internal reality. That always made sense, warm and comforting. But everyone else's reality was cold comfort. And so I never had much use for that reality, as it has never really been an ally to me, more like a kissing-cousin. It was, (as it is still, sometimes) full of pain, fear, and countless enemies. And as enemies they always seemed willing to whittle you down, take what is yours, and urinate on your torn and tattered sense of self.

I know only, that I was afraid, I didn't understand my lessons, such as maths or English, and could not perform at p.e. I was a true pariah, different, because of what I know now to be mild learning difficulties, and my then serious inability to comprehend my fellows. The tutors frowned and chastised me, calling me "Lazy, stupid, useless, good for nothing", etc, etc, not all of them did so, some were sympathetic, and understanding, but there were the others, who made my life miserable. An already fragile soul was reduced to ashes under the malevolent gaze of my person demons.

I have had problems with learning ever since I can remember, a loyal companion, always there, although not as cuddly as a cat or dog. No, this pet was cruel, and the repercussions of its companionship harrow me to this day, in nightmares, from which I awake, in a cold sweat. I was a slow child, understanding simple concepts a true challenge for me.

And in those days it really seemed there was very little hope for me. In fact, it is a perception that has only recently started to fade. Recent years have hacked and chipped away at this harsh presence in my life. But back then things were different. Teachers would shake their heads, and summon my mother to the school. Help would be promised but never arrive. I was bad enough to not succeed, but good enough to not be given help. This has never made any kind of sense to me. I spent time in special schools, infant and primary, but by the time I went into senior school, this help disappeared, and I was stranded, figuratively. I was stuck on a strange island that was named "hopeless". I could not read well till about ten or eleven, or understand how to tell the time. This wasn't real problem for me, especially the 24-hour clock. I just didn't get it. And shoe laces. Shit, that was bad.

I cringe, and fight the tears as they roll down my cheek as I type this, the memories painful and overwhelming, the loneliness of a small boy, the terror and confusion I felt, like an immense weight on my back. There was not much hope then, not for me. Even as a child, I felt inferior, and less than others. I honestly was a late developer. Maths has never made sense, and at the age of 26 I still cannot divide or multiply too well at all. Times tables were never really my things. But I have adapted as I got older, learnt coping mechanisms, and it's nowhere near as noticeable now. I was late developing, yes, but I've caught up, I have definitely discovered strengths, and I am now beginning to accept my limitations without anger or frustration.

I guess it's partly due to new found emotional maturity. I had gained an acceptance of myself. This is new, and I still struggle. But for the most part I am at peace with myself in that way at least. But it has not always been that way. I guess that I have to admit to myself that I wasn't very popular at for the most part of my schooling. It always seemed that I was doomed to be a loner, forever apart from the crowd.

It hurts to remember. I can see where it started to go wrong, and what led me to be here. Wish I could change it, I really do. God Please forgive my selfish ramblings, I am feeling sorry for myself as I write this passage. As I take a deep breath, I ground myself, and the tightness in my chest begins to fade away. And that allows me to continue.

"I did not hang with the boys" And maybe that was no bad thing, as most of them I think, ended up in bad situations, even worse than what was to come for me. I was a victim of fear, of an inferiority complex, of brow beatings at home, and laughter from my peers. I was to encounter abuse, sexually, physically, and intellectually, emotionally. I wonder now, if they were victims too, and they were lashing out, attempting to assert themselves, have identity, be feared, as they were taught to fear. They knew I think that if you make others fear you, you don't have to fear them. If you are yourself feared then attacks are that much less likely to occur. This is a philosophy I have always felt uneasy with. It is somewhat morally ambiguous.

Even as children, we are taught lessons in social control and domination, ye gods, what are we doing to the young? What are we doing to society? I know not. But I can tell you, more than a couple of my peers ended up in jail, or homeless, because they became even worse as they got older. Giving up, stealing for drugs, until they were kicked to the curb, and abandoned. My heart aches for them, as I knew pain, back then. And so did the rest of them.

I was weak, but I wasn't cruel, and some of them had a rather serious little predisposition to do harm to others. They got worse. I guess I honestly thought I was a nicer guy coz I didn't take my shit out on others. Can you imagine that arrogance? I was cosy within the knowledge that I was at least, a good boy. I feel sick, wretched with the fact I had that mindset. Programmed to accept bullying, and be content, because I was deserving of it. I was a good boy to watch and wait, for the next attack. This mental self programming was ridiculous. My own righteousness dammed me. How arrogant was I then? I am angry with the young me for ever being so foolish. But hindsight is an easy and wondrous thing.
 That's what it all boils down to.

I don't think I was nice, at all. Maybe, I just didn't have the guts to do that? Ii didn't have it in me to hurt others. To be that calculating and to realise being feared meant safety from harm. On reflection I don't think I am any better a human being. I wanted to be unleashed, parading, braying, asserting MY dominance, coming out of the shadows, without fear. And as ashamed as I am of this fact, I still want to lash out in pain. I do not usually, but they had the guts to do so. I have at times, and have always suffered guilt so intense I felt I was dying. They were true to themselves, whereas I hid in the shadows, suffering in silence, being trampled as a door mat.

Not so with these guys. I want to lash out, but I cannot, because it feels alien, wrong. It leaves a bad taste in my mouth, harsh and metallic. I have always felt such guilt and shame, all through my life, and I am not sure why.

But it is impossible for me to wilfully hurt someone else, due to this all consuming guilt. Perhaps that isn't a bad thing, in that sense. But it cripples me and prevents me from living a real life. I was judged as being too quiet, feminine, and strangely enough, unthreatening. Because of this, I was prey. To not be the prey, you had to be a predator. At my old school, Mundella Community College it always seemed that if you were a little bit nasty, you were respected, or maybe just feared. Either way, it seemed better than being bullied at the time as I recall.

But I didn't have that in me. Weakness or strength, I still cannot decide. I have that dark desire within me, but it has never been unleashed. Snapping and snarling, biting and clawing, its way into the light of day. It remains chained, deep inside me. I didn't spray paint the teachers cars, didn't attack those with special needs, or threw rubbish at unsuspecting passers by as others did on a daily basis. These things did not impress me, and that marked me. It made me in their eyes, "weird."

That and the fact I sat on my own, away from the others. It was because I felt inadequate, unsure of myself, and I knew, I couldn't cope with the schoolwork, and this depressed me. I didn't know I was depressed but yeah, I was. I can clearly see that now. And I wonder why this was never picked up by others, why I was never seen, never helped. If only I had called one of the help lines for children and gotten help then. The abuse I suffered at 11 has set me back, and whilst I have had much therapy, I have never ever really discussed all that in-depth. It has always been skirted around because the therapist felt I was unready, or before that, I never revealed it.

This needs addressing at some point. But for now, back to My Childhood, back to School where I did not fit in. So I was apart from the others, and this got worse as I went on. I never did understand the other children, couldn't relate to them, at all. I had difficulties integrating, and I still do. I had no confidence, and it's bloody hard to be assertive when you loath yourself!

So as it later became obvious, and painfully so at that, I was quite an introvert, and didn't like sports (couldn't run to save my life, didn't like the javelin, and sure as hell couldn't play football) and so didn't meet the schoolboy stereotype of what a "bloke" should be. And so I attracted unwanted attention, getting called names like "Poof" and "Nancy boy" none of them very original, but all bloody painful to hear, and get called.

 Then there were the others, such as "dick licker", and "shit-shoveler" etc. it now occurs to me, how did they know about such things, where did they learn these terms? I am sure it started at home. Not a good education, or start to life, I think. It was not Very original terminology. Although it was quite creative really. That is if you think about it. A real intellect behind that one. What seems deliciously ironic to me now, and more than a little funny, is back then, I had no **IDEA** about my sexuality! All that soul seeking Wondering if I was gay or bisexual. Happily I know now I am bisexual, not restricted by thoughts of gender or sexual straightness. I like both sexes, and I think that's ok. But I didn't then, indeed I didn't until recently. But more on that later.

But as a child that was what they called me. It seems they were more aware about the beating of my own heart than I was! God, how weird is **THAT?** All I knew back then was, I admired a strong body, wanted to experience that musculature, and didn't really like the girls overly-much at all. But I did not realise I was any the different for that. Well, nice of them that eh? Educating me, like. Yeah' right. **NOT.** And so the beatings began, as they started to follow me home from school, ambushing me in gangs, jumping out of the bushes etc. if I left the house and people saw me, I knew, just knew that I was going to be attacked.

Oh yeah, was **THAT** fun. But you **CAN** tell that I am being sarcastic here, right? They seemed to think "pick on the Nancy boy coward" and the horrible thing is, I let them do it, for so long. Oh yes, I was cowed by them, and I was afraid for my life, in mortal fear, most of that time. From the age of 12 or so, I was in constant fear. I remember when I got to 14' it got so bad I used to hide out in the toilets for a couple of hours, and I did that for **MONTHS.** I would sneak out, and go the long way home, running, never stopping, until I got there.

I did this, so that I wouldn't be seen and then attacked. It never occurred to me to try and take them on. It was probably a good thing too. I started to pull up my hood over my head, even in summer, in the strange belief that if I couldn't see them, then they couldn't see ME. Of course, this strange sight only provoked them to attack and mock me, resulting in my running, and that causing them to chase me al the more. I think it was something to do with feeling invisible to my parents.

I remember feeling that they could not see me, as a person, not the real Adam, but only my problems, you know, I think I was spot on. But acting in that way, well it makes you stand out. And so over time this frankly odd behaviour started to become known. It was equally amusing and frustrating from the bullies in equal measure, I am sure. So they started to make an example of me all the more' it was an exciting thing for them, I was scared, so I am pretty sure for them it was a case of "look what we are making Adam do" "what else will he do?" they were in complete mastery of me, mentally and physically. I was chained to fear. And I don't think I have ever completely broken those chains.

So I used to hide in these grotty awful toilets near the hardware classes, because no one ever used them, because they were so awful. But a bully happened to find me there one day when he was sniffing gas in the cubicle next to me. Of course he told others, and they delighted in locating me because they had tried to find me in the lunch room and in the playground. And so they used to go around each cubicle, knowing I hid there regularly. Banging on them, and screaming my name, violence and menace in there voices. Looking under each door, spitting in at me, throwing in used condoms, cigarette butts, kicking at the doors, threatening me, all shitty scary stuff.

Then when I came home, they would chase me, sometimes just some of the way, sometimes all of the way home, and they would be standing there, getting a big laugh out if it. Bloody hell, it was shit. Yeah, it was crap. But I dithered, and I cowed, and I let them win. So it got worse. A hell of a lot worse. Running from the bullies never helps. I think I bullied myself mentally, as indeed I still do. There voices still resound in my head, even though I can no longer place faces or remember names. The voices live in me still. As do the voices of anyone who has ever shouted at me or hurt me in any way. The whole lot of them drown out my own feeble shouts for help in a terrible cacophony of sound. I am not always entirely conscious of this happening, but it does.

I thought I was thick, stupid, ugly, because I had to wear Glasses, etc. so I gave up and gave in, because inside my head, I thought they were right, and I deserved it. No. it's more than that. I felt I knew they were right. So even now, I will not wear glasses even though I am very short-sighted, because deep down I still believe I will be attacked if I am even slightly different. Of course this is wrong, but I didn't realise this at the time. Well anyway, there is a park near where I used to live, down on the Morton estate.

And it was surrounded by high bushes, and it had been a refuge for me, from the bullying at school, and fear of not being wanted at home. This was actually probably much worse that the physical bullying itself. Though I know cruelty wasn't meant, I felt worthless and stupid, unlovable. I know my parents wouldn't have wanted me to feel this way, but it was the case. Although it was most likely meant in a constructive way, the things I was told were hurtful. It they were entirely verbal. At least that was the case at first.

It was only right at the end before I left home this changed. It was "you are not my son"

"be more of a man, boy" and "you are stupid" my father was not ever terribly supportive of me it has to be said. I have always had the sense he didn't approve of me, or particularly like me much, due to things he said and did, which I do not feel able to discuss in this book. These things are private family matters and so are best left out. But the relationship between us has always been rocky for various reasons, and got worse as I got older, coming to a point, where it was decided by my mum and me it was best that I got a flat of my own. Things were really getting better between us, not exactly close, but closer. But we aren't talking as of the time of writing this book. He wont talk to me as he doesn't agree with my left wing stance on the world, he wont talk to me because I am bisexual and embarrassed about that, and feels I am dirty filthy animal, that I have shamed his family ancestry that I have mad him a laughing stock amongst his war friends, that I have dishonoured him in some way. He is extremely homophobic, and some of that is his age I think, but another part of it is that he truly doesn't see all people as equals. This saddens me but it is a fact. I am starting to get to the stage where I am switching of, because he has never acted particularly loving and caring towards me. And that hurts me deeply, a wound I cant see healing anytime soon, because he doesn't see me as a human, as a person, he sees me as property, chattel, and this isn't right. I love him, and one would hope that he loves me, but he has never shown that really, and as a child he frightened me with his attitudes and behaviour, the things he said, and did.

Particularly In the months just I moved out. All this is the truth, and I know that would hurt him to read. He didn't mean me harm. But he hurt me. He did. He would hate to read this he would call me a liar, but it is the truth. And it needs to be told. So I can continue my growth into a whole person. Perhaps then I can even make him proud of me for achieving things in life that I cannot do whilst I am chained by fear and depression and this very real hate of myself. I hate my face and my hands my body my personality. I hate my own life. And I know this is a sin. I know that I should rejoice in life because god created me to do so. But it is hard.

It was not entirely my parents fault. I know that. They just couldn't understand my terror, struggles to learn, to associate with others of my age, to act like all the rest/ I as never able to integrate due to what went on inside my head. I was always a seriously troubled child, things in my mind, bullying at school, fear at home. They didn't understand me I don't think, and I believe that it angered and disgusted them, my father especially. I guess he was ashamed of me. Anyway, it was all "why hide, fight boy, hit them back". I remember my mother once told him it as different in their day, the laws now were different. That if he did now what he did as a child he would be serving a long prison stretch. This shows you a little of his character. Strong wild, strong minded, forceful and frightening, although he may not have intended to be. As a child he could flay me alive just by looking at me. He didn't have to speak, although he did, and it burned. He was a rough one even as a child. He was bullied so he became one to prevent that. Much like those bullies I described earlier.

I know I was not an easy child to bring up. The strain of having a boy who was afraid of other kids, couldn't learn too well, didn't get sports and who hid in his room, I guess he couldn't cope with it. I wasn't anything like him, and I'm still not, I guess. I am a liberal, I fight human rights violations with amnesty international and want to serve the public, he thinks this is weak and I should serve myself. He was bullied but he fought back, and beat them up, was aggressive, and they were afraid of him. This is not the path my life has taken.

Add to this the fact he was very, very talented, and intelligent. When he was a young man, 20-ish or so, he won a scholarship to Gateway College. Which wasn't so common then, it was a place that was at the time quite posh. What I mean by that is, the kid's parents had money, he had none, was clothed in rags almost, and so he was bullied. But he was a real fighter, and so he finds it distressing I could not be more like him. Be a fighter.

It was constant warfare, my childhood, and I hated it, and hated myself, was full of self loathing. And because I was certain he hated me, for various reasons I will not go into here, as I don't think it serves any purpose,(not any positive one in any case), I started to dislike him also, the more he pushed the more I withdrew. This only made him angrier and more aggressive, and so I withdrew all the more. This happened right up until I just had to leave. But understand, I love my father dearly, and want very much a strong and loving relationship with him. I can't stress that enough. I began to distance myself from my father, as you do when the one you love, abuses you, as he did. You need to understand, bullying comes in many forms, and my father was as big a bully as the ones I faced at school, and in the community.

Just because I have a little insight as to why I am as I am, does not make it any easier. So It was here I started to get ill I think, self harm thoughts first started to form, thoughts of suicide first started to filter into my conscious mind, but I quickly blocked them out, frantic with worry, scared of this way of thinking.

I started to get angry really angry, but I allowed it all to go on, never challenging them. Not really knowing how. I didn't even try, not until I was 16, near the end of my schooling. So then it got to the stage where I was hunted to that park, my refuge, and I would be ambushed by others who had run the quick way around, just so they could ambush ME! I was so predictable. I couldn't have been any more transparent. I was only poor little weak and pathetic Adam. I was only the boy who couldn't fight back.

Until the day that I threw a bully into the wall behind him, and kicked him in the groin, cracking him in the nose, as my dad thought me. I left him there, against the bench, near the school gym, and what sickens me now, I was proud, I was actually proud. I knew my father would not in respect, and at least for a time, I was safe at home. I became a predator, and so could not be prey… see how I was conditioned by my experiences? I admit it, excited that I got them back a bit.

I am Ashamed of it now' I know better, and I guess I did then, but anger got the better of me. They didn't all believe I had done that, but they began to become unsure about me, I had always been so meek before. Another time, I pushed my fingers up a guy's nose, and pushed his head back away from me, and shit, that hurt him, I reckon. In short, I had seen little of violence, and I eventually learnt to use violence. But I also learnt how to use reason, to talk things through in my own clumsy fashion, to use distraction because I didn't relish the alternative of violence in any form. I am a pacifist and proud of it.

But back then I did use violence during a period in my life when things were unbearable. Later on I lost my ability to be calm and I continued to be verbally aggressive for five years of therapy and mental distress. It's only of late, this past year or so I can take people being aggressive without verbally flailing back at them. I occasionally have lapses but these are rare. Usually these occur only with my father. I'm not proud of myself of all of this you know, it caused me lots of problems later on, guilt, confusion, problems with identity, and you will just have to trust me on this.

As I have already said, my bullying was not just due to my inability to act the same as them, and the fact that I did not get the same kick out of being cruel and part of the in crowd as they did. But also due to my lack of sporting prowess, and the fact that I really didn't get school much at all. My learning difficulties were pretty obvious. Of course, I know why now, I have dyslexia and the maths equivalent of this which is called dyscalculia, which pretty much explains it all. I was not thick or stupid, or "slow" I merely had a condition, which is now commonplace and it should have been picked up then but was not.

I was told I was thick, and my parents told I was "a slow child". My classmates teased me mercilessly, and the other kids beat on me. It was funny for them to pick on a guy who didn't have a clue, about what was happening to me, mentally at all. I was suicidal, angry, and depressed, although I didn't realise that at the time. Nobody did, but I was this way from the age of 15 or so, not from the age of 20 when I was first seen for these issues. I know it now however. I guess that's the gift of hindsight for you. But back to the bullying. No matter what the cause is, be it due to learning issues, sexuality, race, sex, whatever, it is far better Instead to be assertive, rather than aggressive, say no, and stand up to them. Bullies focus on fear, they smell it, like a shark can smell blood, and they feed on it, just like an animal.

Question them, challenge their viewpoint, use logic, and take the focus off you as a victim, because most bullies are not very well developed emotionally. Indeed I am sure that's why they bully, and so you can defuse the situation. I learnt that too late. I Wish I had learnt it earlier. I learnt it at the tender age of 21.

And I am only 26 at the time of writing this. I am not old at all in that sense. And I find that very sad. I have not been the most emotionally self-aware human being that is for sure. But I am on the right track now, and I guess that's something. But that wasn't the end to my being bullied, and it wasn't the end of my fear and confusion, lack of identity either. Oh No. In fact I still struggle with assertiveness' and all that to this day. When I left school I left with extremely bad grades, because I was NOT very good at school. I was not at all academic.

As I have already said I wasn't good at sports, science, maths, etc, so my parents gave me a hell of a lot of grief, and didn't even try to hide their disappointment. Nor did they hide their embarrassment, Anger, from me at all. Seeing this in them, seeing how I made them feel was soul shattering. It was a time of multiple hells, life was unbearable, shame guilt and anger followed me as if an entourage back then. As they do now, fully grown, and leering, breathing over me with fetid breath .Childhood was not good for me, then, Waves of terror permeated the air around me, not knowing how they would act towards me, and the fear was very real, very tangible.

The weeks after were very, very tense. I was very down, amazingly low, washing, eating; all seemed superfluous, and meaningless. As indeed they still do. I think my depression started fully about here, I have suffered with it consistently since childhood, not acknowledging it, but it was there, in the back of my mind, shadow like, and coiled, ready to pounce, and render me limb from, bloody limb.

It was a gremlin, lurking, chitterling and giggling, as it did its insidious work, laying doubt and confusion within my easily influencable mind. Because of my lack of perceivable ability, in any area, because of this, my parents would not even consider letting me go to college. Please try to see, to Understand, my parents were and still are really, quite poor, and could not afford to waste money on me doing college, they knew, without a doubt, I would fail them, and myself, And not only would they have very little money left to survive on my fathers war pension and the housing benefit their only source of money, they would be landed with the shame of having a dumb, backward, retarded and useless son.

My dad wanted his family line untarnished, and having succeeded in his own life, against incredible odds, he didn't want me being a fly in his ointment. As bitter as I am, as angry as this dismissal makes me, at the horrendous contempt he showed me day in day out, I can at least partly, understand this. He has suffered his own pain, gone through things I can only see in my worst nightmares, and this partly explains his actions. They don't excuse them, nothing can, but it does give an insight into how it all occurred.

My track record up-to that point had not been great, I had had many problems, due to being slow at learning. We now know I am dyscalculic, which explains my serious problem in comprehending the meaning of numbers, their functions. My father still looks down on me even though I have explained all this; my brother once told me I was finding excuses. Though I now think he has got a better insight.

And also the fact I am dyslexic, and mildly disphraxic. "Dysphraxia" is perhaps better known as "clumsy child syndrome." For-armed with this knowledge, looking back, I see where I stumbled, but look at me now, and not much of that remains visible. I have begun to transcend that curse, people are seeing me for me, and this is good. But back then. People had no faith in me. No faith in my ability to persevere… my parents, they doubted me, as indeed, they still do. They didn't consider looking for a grant or money to assist me; I guess they had not been used to thinking in that way, being working class and not doing FE. Also my mother made it clear I should not push my limits, to except I was less than my fellows,

A pallor shade compared to them, their brilliance outshining my faint glow, branding me a no go, in her eyes at least. She had no belief, in me, no desire to push me, she was content to let me wallow, believing I was nothing, and not trying to do stuff she had raised me to accept, stuff I wasn't able to. She was doing all this out of love. But she was hurting me by doing this. Loving me enough to try and spare me pain, but wounding me by not hiding her doubt of me as a person. My parents were becoming very distant and accusing parents. I feel they couldn't handle me. My father is 74 and my mum 67 at the time of writing this and I am 26.

They couldn't handle me then, and they can't handle me now. The subtle contempt blossomed and bloomed into all out warfare, father became a figure to fear, rather than someone I felt sheltered by. He became a distant figure, he became my obsession, because he didn't show affection or love, I tried to earn it, and of course I couldn't, because he couldn't give it to me. And so, he became my entire world, and it became an altogether darker place. I began considering cutting first, around the time I was about 14, fifteen, coming up to leaving school, because of where my age fell in the year. It was to be a couple of years, before I first slit open my arm, but the seed, was planted, left to germinate, and grow. This poem that I had written shows how I felt and still feel even now, that I was just a child. Just a child, scared and frightened, not to blame, and now I have scratched and clawed my way to adulthood, I am treated that way still, even though I am not that child. And the pain this causes is excruitiating. So here it is. "A child".

A Child

A Child'
It is born.
 And what does it feel?
Pain and Confusion.

A Child'
It grows.
Now what does it feel?
Fear and Bewilderment.

A Child'
Beaten, Abused.
Raped.
So how should it feel?
Scared, and Angry.

How the fuck would you feel?

A Child'
Flung into the World,
Left alone,
To break, to Cry, to Die.

I sit here,
Feeling Hurt and Used.
I truly believed in you.
The liars, the carers,
 The good-
And so I thought,

 The nice people.
The
Establishment.

What did I need?
Safety, and Caring.

Maybe even love, of a sort.
But what do I know,
 really?
After all,
 I'm nothing to you.
In your eyes,
What am I?

Nothing but a child,
Still.

 I feel angry now. Seriously bloody angry, and this is frightening is for me as I have learnt to suppress anger because it has always been dangerous for me. Other people's anger has resulted in pain for me many times in the past but I cannot hide my own any longer. I fear this is going to be a bit of a rant. But it needs to emerge I feel.

This book is about my discovery and I am experiencing these thoughts fully for the first time. It really is hard for me to write this, to go through this, so please bear with me. I can only hope God can forgive me for this. These feelings are beyond anger I think. I think this is rage and that is a sin. I was told things as a child that made me feel so utterly worthless and pathetic and unloved that I think it has had some effect on my behavioural and thinking patterns. I am not blaming it all on others here; just acknowledging it played its part. Enough said.

 Just before I left home there was a lot of tension in the air. A lot of tension and stress in the household, seemingly because I wasn't a normal child. And this of course affected them. My dad told me word to this affect whilst my mum was out at the shops on numerous occasions. He said things like that, and then they expected me to perform flawlessly, and go through education, get a job, live the life of a perfectly well adjusted individual. At least that's the way it seemed to me. He meant me know harm, I believe this, but it was done nonetheless.

 I do not want this to impact on the relationship between the two of us, and I will not ever stop caring for him, and loving him. But these things happened. But I could not live that way, and I cannot because you I am a little damaged I think. I am recovering, but the mental distress I carry, the guilt shame, dread, fear and sense of nothingness within me, these all cause me to fail, and because I have ended up with physiological problems, then ended up in therapy, on benefit, unable to hold down a job, or perform in education, I feel as if most of my family think that I am lazy, a good for nothing lay-about who just wants money for nothing, wanting only to rip of the system, and the good people who pay their taxes. Most of my family have not said this, although there has been certain people who did, and it's not easy to forget that kind of grudge. This really was not something I particularly wanted, know what I mean? It isn't fun, being stuck in therapy, or being in hospital, not earning a wage, living off of benefits, feeling you area complete and utter failure, a scourge on the face of normal society. I often felt I should just crawl away and die, because at least then nobody would be stuck with the burden that is me. And you know what? I still often feel that way. No matter how hard I try and shift this feeling, its deeply entrenched, and I imagine it will take many years of self discovery to alter this. And it may never go entirely, in actual fact.

The people who said that have forgotten I think, and as for the rest of them, they deny that in my case, but it was said even if they no longer remember saying it. My brother has done this too, with me, though he has forgotten, and things are so much better between me and him now. I am very, very sure now that my parents, dad particularly did not mean the pain he caused me, I am sure. But he was always very quick to lay the blame' "you never succeeded well at school" "weren't good at sports couldn't make friends".

My father's mentality was "Why are you always doing this? "Always forcing me and your mum to come to the school because another teacher had issues with you" and also "why can't you learn/ what's wrong with you? Why are you so useless?"

And of course, we cannot forget this next one – my mum and dad told me very early on about nine or ten about my half brother s and sisters and that they had had me in an attempt to unite the two sides of the family my mums children and my dads, by having little old me. And I have always felt bad for not achieving this. I'm sure it isn't what they intended me to feel, for sure. But I do. Even now. But was this my fault really? So did I cause my mom (who I so dearly very much love, by the way, more than I could ever, ever say- to give birth to me?) Did I decide that they would call me "Adam – First Born "Did I make the decision to have a child to unite two utterly different and dissolute families? Did I decide to give **MYSELF** such a role? The answer to that of course, is a resounding NO

It wasn't just that though. It was the things my father said when he was angry which I have always, always carried with me, I never forgot the tone, the look on his face, the feelings of dismissal I got when he said them. He probably didn't mean it but his rage suggested he did. These were the kind of things I got, and these are the milder ones:

 "**YOU** aren't **MY** son, no son of mine would act the way **YOU** do" "It's **YOUR** fault that I am getting and your mum is too, and we cannot cope with a fully developed, energetic young man of 26 years of age, you tire us out, you bring us down – and its your fault." So, did I ask for this kind of thing? And did I ask to be told as a young 16-year-old boy this was the reason he was alive? That I was here for this purpose only? The answer to all of these questions is No.!! But it's only at the age of 26 that I am starting to realise this one. It's a little too late for this, I think.

I've been told I am suffering with post-traumatic stress disorder, with borderline personality disorder also. I've been wondering why for years since. Well there it is in all its ugly glory. The burden I have been carrying for almost ten years now. I am the one left with all of the Anger and the pain. And I find it is forgivable to rant. I can forgive myself this luxury. This is what happened, what really occurred. And so I left school, at 15 since my birthday fell funny within the school year. My father will be very angry with this, but hopefully he will see that it's not just the stuff between us I talk about here in this book, its all the issues, everything that has hurt me for so long.

He is a immensely private ma, and hates the idea of my discussing my issues in his book anyway, due to the usage of the pick family name. But this is my story, and I am sure he realises how much I love him, and this isn't meant to hut anyone. It's merely my journey of self discovery, looking at what has affected me, and how I can develop as a human being, and as a person. This is a period of growth for me, as painful as this is for everyone, both me, and those who know and care for me.

 So this was my childhood up until this very point. Then it happened. School ended, and home began fully, same pain, differing intensity. As I got older I was able to put a name to it – loneliness, the loneliness of one who does not understand those around him, the pain of whom he was, and who was abused constantly, in differing ways, the pain of one who had come to forget the meaning of "kindness". And "love". That is the pain I felt, and to some extent, still feel.

It was just after this point in time, just before my 17th birthday I did cut, I did self-harm, I was full of need, a need to let go everything that was building within me. I was fragile, in emotional pain, and I couldn't stand it, I just couldn't. The need erupted, blasting open, beginning in earnest, carving the secret language of fear upon my scared and battered carcass. Hiding in the changing rooms at work, cutting myself with a blade I hid in my locker. Eventually being discovered, and mocked. It was shortly after I had my breakdown, and left, destined for a year in FDL, therapeutic community. But this leads me back to the beginning, childhood and not knowing what the bloody hell was going on with me.

Because its only now' when I look back at my childhood I see why I felt that way, I did not understand anything, none of what was happening within me, but now, as an adult, I can see it all clearly, with clarity, and it **HURTS.** God' it **HURTS** so badly I don't want to wake up again sometimes. I left home at 17 because' because my father and mother could not get a supported/ warden assisted bungalow whilst I lived at home, so they cajoled, me into agreeing to leave, and I did.

They thought, I think it was because i saw the point they were making, even though that wasn't the main reason,(and I have always known that, there were other issues) no the reason I left in truth was it was all making me so desperate to go of guilt and fear, that I was willing to get a council flat away from them. This is true. But there were other reasons.

Again this may cause hurt, and I don't want that, I so desperately don't want that, but I cant hold all this stuff inside any longer, I need to work out who I am, what im about. What has affected me in this way, so I can deal with my issues. And there are many, most of them completely unrelated to family. I am still quite immature, developmentally I feel. i have come on a long way, but I still have a way to go. But things were even worse as a child, emotionally speaking. When I left home, I put on the show of being able to cope, and even looking forward to it because I was angry. But I wasn't ready, no way, it was obvious. I think my sister was annoyed at the fact I was being asked to go, I think I remember her indicating that, but I am not sure.

 But the fact remains that I was still far too immature to live and survive alone. But my mum and dad did try and help with money, quite a bit (for which I will always be most grateful) and furniture and bits and bobs. They helped a lot, but I have this deeply felt suspicion its because my mum felt guilty that I was leaving home when I was so obviously not coping at work, or in my life, daily. (Indeed it would only be 18 months before I was admitted into the therapeutic community, because of an emotional issue caused by relations with someone that went awfully wrong). But mum and dad did help me on quite a few occasions, and I did at these times felt cared for deeply for,

I feel sick, and faint. Remembering all this hurts so much, I am crying as I write this, I am in floods of tears I want to punch something, it hurts that much.The pain radiates outwards. My heart pumps madly in my chest, threatening to burst from its cavity, to lie bleeding its precious fluids into the green plush piles of my carpet, giving it a darker, hue.

The pain is familiar, one that I have felt, pretty much everyday, as long as I can remember. The pain of one, who knows he is alone, lost to the world, a misfit.It has different levels and intensities, of course. Sometimes, a sharp keening wail, sometimes a muffled sob. As the pain intensifies, becoming akin to that of a bad tooth, but running the entire length of the body, and amplified, a hundred, thousand times.
I am assaulted by memories. I adore my mother, but as a child I was afraid of her too, mainly because she was so protective, so sure I would fail, wasn't as good as other kids, not capable that she was so negative and told me not to try, almost encouraging me to give up.

This was because she didn't want me to be hurt, because she loved me, and I know that. I really do. But that is not the point; I guess… it was awfully placating and heavy, like drowning in honey at times, and then being abandoned cold at others.
I was always so scared, so full of doubt as a kid, scared to say boo to a goose, in case I was pounced on and attacked. Even then I had a deep rooted sense of being substandard, and school life only increased this fact. I was called a "scrubber2 indicating I was fit only to scrub others boots and I was avoided and spat on like I was dirt. It seemed that there was no escape from the torment that was then my life.

The rape, when I was eleven or so, was still an unseen that was to become an unwanted presence, pressing on the wall of my mind, threatening to pierce them, and destroy the fragile balance that was my emerging personality, that was my id, my ego, my essence. "I". The pain began fully then, totally and without any let up around the age of twelve, or thirteen, a sense of being alone, unheard, unseen, unwanted at home, bullied and abused at school, and when that was over, ridiculed, once I got home. My parents are aware of some of what happened to me I think, not the rape, not the sexual abuse, but the bullying at school. Mum tried to stop some of it, but the rest I never told her about. It was too shameful for me. But there are something's at home that bothered me almost as much, cut almost as deeply.

A father that never ever got out of his chair, a father that never ever asked how you were, didn't show any interest in your life, didn't want to talk to you, just shouted at you, and told you to "shut up". That was my dad. He would tell you that in one breathe, and then he would say you were his reason for living, with the next. Taking with one hand and giving with another. Playing mind games and confusing a young man. Everything that happened to me as a child, and a youth took me to the stage that I needed help. I ended up in therapy. And after Two years at FDL, in therapy, a hidden door inside of me just opened.

It was a door into my unconscious mind that I now cannot shut. I have all this stuff streaming out into my head and it's really tough to handle. Unlooked at, and left unchecked, it quickly became am raging maelstrom that I was unable to quell, or get away from. And god, I didn't need that, so help me, I didn't.

Or maybe I should be saying "I don't want this, cannot cope with all of this shit, and I just want it to stop, god, let it stop." But let me explain. I love my mother, and it destroys me to see her bent over, arthritis ripping at her from within, stripping her ever day, and in pain constantly. Add to that her diabetes, and heart problem, she doesn't have it easy, not at all. I would gladly give my Life for her, if she could only be made whole and happy again. Likewise with my Dad. I also love him deeply, and want him in my life, healthy, loving, and excepting me as I am. But this is just a pipe dream, and it cannot happen.

He is on oxygen, 17 different types of medication, and nebuliser, wheezing, unable to breathe. He is in a constant living death. He has no quality of life, and it kills me to see. He hurt me, but I love him. He is my father, I can do little else. I would do ANYTHING to be able to fix him, make him well, whole again. Better. I feel this is my entire fault. Illogical, I know, but love doesn't hold any logic, does it? He is my dad. And I love him. At his point, I pause, for I must. Because I am filling my mind with imaginary thoughts of candyfloss, fairground rides, and the more real, memories of the positives I have known, friends, the taste of popcorn, beer, memories of distant laughter, and more recent smiles, before I can continue.

There is only so much pain I can bare to recall at once, as indeed, any human mind can tolerate, this is what I feel. But now, I must tell you more of my poetry. So that brings me almost up to date, although not quite. I am 26 now. And I haven't worked full time since my breakdown at 19. Therapy unleashed the beast, so to speak, and it now rules me. I have tried College, work, and voluntary work, but was unable to cope with it. So now I have a psychiatrist, who told me I need more therapy, more intense, and more focused, even than **FDL** was, even though the emphasis is different to that placed on you in FDL. And that scares me. I tried the second Admission to **FDL,** and just couldn't hack it. Once it seems, was more than enough for me.

 It just hurt to damn much. My psychiatrist had warned me that the next two years will be absolute hell for me, and yeah, it was. More therapy was to come, later. Well two years later, and it has gotten worse, much worse, but it is starting to abate slightly, and the future is beckoning me onward. But the words of doctor Meakin stay with me still. They were true, honest, and he has never lied to me. And I respect that more than I can say. Not very reassuring though. For some reason I am thinking of my childhood yet again. I had intended to talk about what came next, during work and college but it seems the book is writing itself now, without conscious volition on my part. My unconscious mind seems to have its own story to tell.

I didn't really play as a child, I didn't get that chance. I was an Adult from 16 in the legal sense, but I was an adult in need far before this. At 11 I was an adult fending for myself in a very real sense, all alone. As a child I fantasized I could get a new mum, a new dad, imagining that Patrick and Jamie's mother were my own. I feel bad for this as we are meant to respect our parents. And indeed I do, but they didn't feel like they loved me back then. I can see they do now, but hindsight is a glorious thing is it not? I just wanted to be loved. That's all. And do you know the worst of it? I still do, and sometimes, I still have that fantasy. I want to re-invent myself, have a better childhood, but that just isn't possible.

But I want that normal life, I am striving to correct the gaps in my education, striving to prove to myself that I am not thick or stupid, and so I want to get that degree, live the student life, get a good job and the wage. The car and the house and that perfect 9 till five life. It is a picture of suburban life. Yes. I just want to be bloody NORMAL what ever that means. I want to sort out this shite with my family. I want to be close to mum and dad, and my siblings; I want to get that sense of being a FAMILY.

I just want these experiences of mine to be beneficial to others, people my age and younger need help with this sort of thing, these experiences and feelings. Intervention early on could help to save so many lives, stopping so many suicides, due to heartache and the mental pain. So please, let's look at these things, and nip them in the bud, recognise that things are bad, and prevent them from getting any worse. Let's also provide support for the mums and dads, because surely they don't do this stuff to their kids because its fun, they enjoy it?

No, I don't think so. It's because they strike out in THEIR pain. Their parents may well have done it to them. It's no excuse, but there is always a reason. I believe that. Both sides need counselling, support, but it needs to happen fairly early on, before the problems become irreversible, and the young mind is irreparably damaged, forever. I tried to work after school. Painting and decorating, working in a food factory, working on production lines before training to be a baker. Then, the breakdown. FDL, an attempt to go back to work, a relapse, college, remit, teaching training, computer skills, another relapse, until, I am here now.

I have done another year and a half of therapy, DBT, which helped in some ways not in others. This has now winded down, come to an end, due to personal differences, we couldn't work together me and my therapy. She annoyed me, and I annoyed her. Personality clashes I think. I am so black and white in my world view, and was confused by much, so that ended though I am very thankful for the time we had together. It helped me rely on myself more I think. But doctor Meakin and I both agree I have had quite enough therapy for the time being. And oh, I wholeheartedly agree.

I find myself asking what now, what is to become of me, will I become focused, or will I turn to sand, only to be carried away by the wind? I sometimes doubt very much my ability to survive this time. The fact that I am diagnosed with BPD (borderline personality disorder) stops people from seeing my other issues, symptoms, difficulties, whatever you want to call them.

They are real to me, and even though they may have different causes to others, they are no less a part of me, no less difficult and painful for me to handle but I am also quite hopeful for the future. I can believe now I will survive to move onwards and upwards. But I would like to take a bit of time now to talk about one of my other issues in a bit of depth. My personal Experience of voice hearing isn't a big one, and for this, I am glad. I am not someone who suffers from this phenomenon regularly. If I did, I would die, I feel. I can barely hold onto life as it is, now – let alone if my head was any more garbled than it is now, transmission permanently taken off air, instead of being interced at times, as it is now.

 Luckily my voice hearing does not affect me all the time, as they come and go; they are just a symptom of something deeper rather than a problem in themselves, at least for me. There are others who hear them all the time and I am glad this isn't so for me; I guess I have it pretty easy, when it comes to this. Because I only have to deal with my own issues most of the time, rather than having to deal with voices. But I do hear them, in times of deep and enduring stress, and when I do it's pretty awful. So I want to explain to you know what they say, and how I began to hear them.

My father told me that my mother wished he were dead, so she could marry again and claim his pension. He told me this made him want to die, and that I were the only reason that he continued to live, when he felt he needed to die, because he could no longer cope. And so, I started to hear voices, saying my whole family was evil and should die.

The voices said to my everlasting shame, that my mum was an evil conniving cow, and that she was attempting to poison his tea, so she could claim all his money, and live a new life. This scared me, I had no idea what was happening, I heard these voices in my head, and I was so, so frightened! I thought I was losing my mind, becoming crazy. I know now my voices are me, a part of myself I bury and don't listen to, the dark half of my soul, if you like. I didn't realise that back then though. I was much less self aware at that point in my life. And so I went to my mother and confided what the voices said, and as you can probably imagine, this was NOT a good idea, but then, I was not the sharpest tool in the shed, and just wanted help.

 She told me to shut up, how dare I. If I carried on she would have me locked away, as I was mental. If I said one more word she would disown me. I was so scared to be on my own, like this, without family to back me that I said no more. It dropped bellow the seen and I suffered alone. But it got worse, until there were whispers constantly in my head. I told myself over and over, "It's not real, it's not real. Stop this. Stop this" and in time, they started to fade, only re-occurring in times of real stress. Times where I was at risk of self – harm, or getting flashbacks of rape, and both physical and emotional abuse. They have come back in recent years, most notably in church a month ago when they told me I was not a Christian didn't belong there, should leave and kill myself because I was not loved by god.

Luckily for me I told the church and they have been wonderful. Explaining it all from a Christian viewpoint and it helps to know god does want me and I am loved by him. But at times like these, times of pain, It is then that they come back, telling me to go ahead and kill myself, because I deserve to die, because of what I have done to my mother and father, because I have told tales, told people what happened. I can tell you that most often there are three of them, when I do hear them. This is a fairly recent thing. But sometimes there are so many.

But most often the voices are of my father, brother, and one I do not recognise. I also hear laughter, rolling and booming, malicious laughter, genuine amusement at pain and torment, and I know them all, all the tones, the pitches, all of them. I do not have a lot to say on the subject of voices as I do not here them very often at all, and when I do, It's just mumbling and whispers, like hearing a conversation, but being just out of ear-shot. I do not know about this phenomenon much at all, only having my limited experiences to go on.

The hallucinations are awful, glowing spectres of death, the faces in the walls, twisted in torment, leering out at me. During these episodes things shift and move, the very floor itself changes, shifting, and crawling, the walls dripping and morphing, like running water. The images of people's faces I know distorted, leering, grinning, mocking, combined with laughter often keep me huddled in bed or on the sofa, trembling. Mewing like a child. The professionals put this down to stress, perhaps they are right. They say because I have a certain diagnosis, these things are things I do not experience cannot and yet I do, I know I do, because it is ME who lives with them.

Regardless of the reason I do have these experiences and no one can deny that. Deny my experiences. I refute those who say otherwise. And of late, they are a hell of a lot worse. I know this is stress related, anxiety, fears, paranoia racing out of control, but they are real to me. I am practicing relaxation techniques, using disassociation management skills, and they help keep it in control somewhat. I have been thinking about how I act, how I portray myself, and sometimes that isn't so great. When people understand me, they see why I might act a little crappy, but this isn't good. I am working on filing off my rough edges, correcting aspects of my behaviour, working on becoming a better person. It's hard, but I am getting there. When I feel suicidal it makes me very demanding or at least it did.

For the past four months I have worked at getting back onto my feet, I am back at voluntary work, editing large magazine, as I have previously mentioned for the LGB centre here in Leicester, I have left therapy, I do work for amnesty and CND and Christian aid, I try to think of others, and since becoming a Christian six precious weeks ago I have tried to follow the example Christ set when he died so that I may live, so that all sinners may know the grace of God. And I fall short, very, very short, as we all do, being human and born in sin. But my attitude has changed. Too late perhaps, but change it has. But I am so sorry for what I have done and said in the past.

I used to demand people talking to me, demanding people caring I used to demand understanding. I did not show respect or even friendship to people during this time. I took and did not give. And it is time to repent for that, though I have done in prayer to god many times.

It really saddens me to know that I didn't listen to others I didn't take into account how others felt. I was fighting for survival, in pure survival mode, and it is understandable, but it was not right. I did damage to relationships during this time, lost good friends, perhaps forever. I am so remorseful for this. I am writing this book to but records straight in my mind, and to really show what went on for me. I want to take this time to say I am genuinely very sorry for the things I have said and done whilst desperate. I am very sorry indeed. These things haunt me day to day.

In my 26 years on this Earth I have seen much, done much, not all of it good. And this leads me to thinking about being a young adult, at 26 years old, the changes I have made, the moral changes, the changes I have made by physically actually doing things differently. And the respect I am beginning to earn, people listening to me more. But this wasn't always the case; I have not always been treated with respect, not because I acted badly, because id didn't during the time I am thinking of. It was my naivety, my confusion; really it was purely because I was young.

As if that some how makes up for bad shit, because I was young it didn't matter? That's how it often felt. So, I want to talk about something that is very close to my heart: Respect. Or the lack of it. Not because I want to brow beat or punish because I think misunderstanding makes things harder for all concerned. Young people have issues too, lots of them, and I think older people often forget how bad they felt as young people. We all need respect. Familiarity breeds contempt' and both other service users and the staff I have had dealings with, from varying organisations, can suffer from some kind of "mental blank" when it comes to appreciating each of us for our merits. The act of recognising each of our "worth" and appreciating each and every one of us for whom we are. That's not always an easy one, I know. But it comes down to having respect. I hate it when service user's turn on each other, we should have a bit more understanding of each other than that. After all we have some common ground. It seems to me, that there are divides that run very deep,

Dispelling the myth that we are united in our pain, having this as a common bond which makes us able to empathise with each other, making the suffering of intense emotional distress at least a partially beneficial experience, by us forming strong bonds with each other. This can happen, but it doesn't always. Unfortunately having issues does not always bring us together. When we have issues with trust abuse and anger, it's an explosive combination and people do rub each other up the wrong way. It is life.

But with respect, it's fairly easy to respect and tolerate each other, even if we cannot be best buddies. Without it however life can be hell. There are still those out there who judge on sex, colours, creed, age, and sexual preference. Even when you all have a common bond, which is having been through deep shit, and been generally screwed around by the fucking system. Just surviving shit doesn't make us decent people. That must come from within, I guess. It is a fact that being younger than most others who belong to user-led groups can indeed lead to a gross miss-underestimation of our individual talents, and our ability to comprehend and understand and to contribute to the causes under consideration.

I find that when we make a point, contribution, or in any way try to exert our talents, making a difference, most often, you make a point, explain your idea in a fairly rational and sometimes inspirational way, and you are met with blank faces, scorn derision or mute nodding' people making it perfectly clear that you are NOT valued, But adding insult to injury, they PRETEND to value you, paying lip service to you, thinking that you are actually so dim as to believe their ill concealed lies. It is just them rubbing their shitty attitudes in your face.

BUT WHY DOES THIS HAPPEN? AND WHAT CAN US AS YOUNG PEOPLE DO TO COMBAT THIS APPALING LACK OF UNDERSTANDING AND RECOGNITION?

I want us all to be valued. That's it. That's all I want! Not much to ask … is it? I really don't feel I am asking for a lot here, I am not asking to be a millionaire, or to have the rights to groundbreaking software that's worth millions! I don't want to be another bill gates. I just want what is due me and others without us having to face Smug Condescending behaviour or any other baggage. RESPECT.

That's all. If I truly am not valued, and people judge my contribution to be in valid, then they at least owe me an explanation as to WHY. But I do not deserve to be met with the pompous scorn I have had to put up with in the past. It is a shame that in this day and age, that Age-ism is so rife. Just when we are throwing out the cultural baggage of old, saying NO! To racism, sexism, discrimination against colours or creed, and indeed, religion. Let's get rid of this curse, please let's try to see that young people do have an extremely valid contribution to make to society.

Don't assume we are incapable, or that we are "work-shy" or any of that old ageist rubbish! And I aim this question at young people. Why do we judge EACH OTHER? Why? It achieves absolutely nothing, we need to support and encourage and appreciate one another, because we are valuable, we are important, each and every one of us. It's just that when we are vulnerable, thinks can get into our heads, and affect us, negatively. I think all the negative feedback we get effects us in a highly negative, and highly emotionally charged way! We then lose the will to try, to enhance and improve our own lives, and when this happens, what do we get?

This crap about being layabouts, loving being on benefits, sitting around being lepers and being drained on the fucking system! This is so obviously not the case, at least for the majority of us. Maybe occasionally and in certain cases but mostly NO. We NEED to challenge this, both for ourselves, and for the majority, because we ALL suffer due to this nasty phenomenon.

So to all the organisations who work with young people, open your ears, respect us, don't treat us in a way that we feel you don't care because once you lose our trust, it will not be so easy to earn it back once again. Be warned, in order to contribute, we need to feel worthwhile, and cared for, and when you don't feel that, you just **STOP.**

"A LOT OF YOUNG PEOPLE FEEL THAT THOSE WHO ARE SUPPOSED TO ASSIST AND SUPPORT US DO NOT TRULY CARE FOR, VALUE, OR RESPECT US"

Please do listen to what I have said, even if you do not agree with it' I welcome any feedback, as constructive criticism is a good thing. But be warned that I have my opinions too. But I think that's positive, to have a dialogue where all sides concerned are truly honest with each other. Because that shows mutual respect. Thank-you for listening to me, I apologise if t his little chapter has come across as a rant, as it has not been meant in that way. This book is very organic in that it grows as I type. It really is a living being, given life by my thoughts feelings and beliefs. I do not pretend to be right or even fair all of the time.

These are feelings here. This is how I have felt. I want us all to respect each other. Young people respecting older people. And the older respecting younger, for our respective view points. It is true the way we act does not always encourage respect and it is our job to address that. This subject is very close to my heart, and I really only want to see a positive change in general. **No organisation in particular, is being attacked here, but none are being spared either.**

This next poem expresses fully what I have tried to state in these few paragraphs. The way a professional can make you feel, when you feel dismissed and un-valued, when you have been sure they like, value and respect you, only to cut you dead.. At the time of writing this poem, I was furious, full of riotous fire and wrath, whereas now, I am three years older, and more able to see how it came about. The anger is there, still, but so is understanding. But here it is, in full flow. "Betrayer".

Betrayer

You.
I thought you Knew.
Thought you Cared,
Cared for me.

I thought you were
Different,
Better than the rest,
A gift fro the gods,
Unique. Special.

No. that isn't you.

I thought you Heard the
Cries of pain'
Knew the secret History,

History of my
Heart.
The rending of the soul.

"My Saviour".

No. That isn't you,
Either.

The abuse,
The Physical,
The Mental,
And the sexual,
Too.

It carved wounds,
Deep into my heart,
And if you looked,

Then you would have
 Found them.

But you didn't look did you?
I was just some stupid kid.

Vulnerable,
That's what I was.
Vulnerable.
That's what I am.
Suicidal.
Believe that?

Oh you should.
But No, for if you did that,
 then you would have to admit
 your failure.

I came to you'
Trusting.
And so I started to care'
Foolishly, I cared for you,
Too.

Thought you would care,
Care for me.
Thought you could,

And that you respected me,

For my perceived strength, integrity, and decency
of character.
Pompous of me,
That,
And arrogant,
Too.

No. I will not take this out on myself,
Not now,
Not anymore.

You see only the exterior,
 The young face, strong soul,
Body, and the cheery smile,
 Happy demeanour,
Which is a mask,
Nothing more.

No respect, caring,
Or understanding here.

You say it yourself,
You find it hard; to see me as I am,
 See me as some silly boy,
Like the ones you know.
I am not they,
I am I.

You fooled me.
With you, I am not
Safe.

You Lied.
You Cheated.

I hate you,
You hurt me so much,
And l and love you,
In equal measure.

I want to matter,
 And I need you to care.
 You promised me safety,
 Respect and help,

And gave me nothing.

You.

**So I shall Name you here –
Betrayer.**

Betrayer.

I wrote another poem at the same time, the same evening, this one focusing, on how interactions with those whom I felt didn't value me, didn't respect me, or so the individual inside – back then, I felt reduced to a number, a scribble on a not bad, a date in a filofax. I no longer feel this as intensely as I once did, but it's still there, lurking like a serpent in the background. Insecurity and lack of self worth is a terrible blight.

You Make Me Nothing

**I am a shade,
The Shadow on the wall,
You see me not,
Although I am Here.**

**You hear me not,
Although I speak,**

**And see me Not'
Although I pose, and I prance,**

Dancing to your tune,

I want only your approval,

Just a dog,
Performing tricks,
For a pat on my head.

I have a heart'
You care not for its beating.
I scream Aloud,
But you do not hear.

To You, I am as Nothing,
A mere speck,
Just another name and number,
 A task
A date in your diary.

I am a job,
No longer a person.

My name is Adam,
You do not use it,
You give me another.

One more suited to your view of me,
And my world,
One that reflects the coldness of your heart

Yes, you choose the name'
Your new name
For 'me.
And the name' that you chose?

Nothing.

**Because to you' that's all I am.
And that's what you do.**

You make me nothing.

My Anger has faded, and I see that misunderstandings do occur, people don't listen to each other constantly, and we do rise to anger, and dismiss each other. We shouldn't, but we do. We can only try to rectify this, and I am happy to say, those I had issue with are trying, and do try, and this is all I can ask. For I must try too, to show respect. Show respect to others, to try and understand their feelings, for if I don't do that, I am not doing them justice, not being fair.

Of late I have become so wrapped up in my own pain, and anguish, I have lost sight of the fact that so do those around me, I became conceited and selfish, expecting, almost demanding support from those who were unable to give it, due to being as in need as I was, myself. But still they tried, and tried, until one day, it broke. They hurt me with harsh words, I lashed out in anger, but I am aware now, of what happened, and why. Yesterday it was the 31st of December, it was New Years Eve 2005 and I made a few resolutions.

I resolved to learn to drive so I could work towards my dream of being an ambulance medical technician as well as a part time published writer, I resolved to follow Christ and have faith and give everything I could, and I have made a resolution to take time out to show those in my life how important they are to me, and to make sure I never repeat the mistakes I made again.

To support back, to show I care, to try and have normal conversations, as well as seek support. To give as well as take. Perhaps in this way, I shall become the person they were attracted to, in the first place. I was a giver, decent, I listened, but somewhere along the line, I lost touch with that. I became a taker, and became so used to the support, I took it for granted and that was wrong, it was a mistake. I feel humbled before those who were so wonderful towards me. They have taught me so much about being a man. They have taught me how to be a decent person.

And I guess the simple fact of the matter is, I am in awe of them, I always have been, their talents, skills, and I became jealous, and I squished it down, felt bad, and needed them to show me they cared, because I was so damn insecure, and am still. I behaved in a very bad fashion. Why did I do this, why did I act so wrongly? And why did I act so foolishly? Because I have found that I have a serious flaw. Well I have several, but this is the biggest and worst. What is it? The truth is quite simply im not very good at dealing with how I feel about people. I haven't ever really dealt with them, so when I do, im bad at it.

Though this past five years has moved me on immensely, this past year since august 2005 particularly, im still not so great at making real lasting commitments with folk. Let's talk about the phenomenon of Relationships. You either love them or hate them, or so they say. I seem to do both at the same time. I am reasonably sure my subconscious hates me because it is somewhat of a bastard towards me. Constantly confusing me and baffling me with occurrences I am not equipped to deal with. I am still in puberty, mentally speaking I think.

This is embarrassing, so don't laugh else I shall kick you hard. I have always been rather cack handed in my relational dealings. It is fair to say im rather shit at it really. I am quite charming enough to make people laugh and like me, it's when it gets deeper that the problems occur. It seems I am too deep, and it all goes tits up after that point onwards. It's all a bit crappy really. It's taken me until the age of 26 to realize I have a rather compulsive personality when it comes to forging relationships.

I have a seriously problematic way of getting to know a person, meaning that as I get to know them, I start to invest more and more of my energy into that person, either looking after them, trying to solve or their problems, trying to prevent them from suffering, because of my own pain and distress, my own experiences. I just don't want them to feel as desperate as I have, so I become a confident, listening to all, serving as problem solver, trouble shooter, a sympathetic ear.

Trouble is, I can't switch off from it at all, I think about them all the time, and every time they call, I run to answer. I have supported five or six people this way in the past five years, all of whom have been suicidal, one of whom blackmailed me with those feelings. That is one aspect, the other is I take on a needy role, the more support I am given, the more I need it, I drink it up, and its not enough, so I need more and more, until I stop being a friend, and start being someone who is cared for. I have destroyed two good friendships in this way, and as soon as I realized this, what was occurring, I went straight back into the caring role. It seems obvious to me now, I have an addictive and compulsive way of coping.

I either give everything, or take all I can…. There doesn't seem to be any level ground. I am a black and white thinker, I always have been, and the shades of grey don't exist for me, and I find this very difficult, as do those around me from time to time. Mainly, I hide this by humor; I can make people laugh, so they forget…. I think I need to matter, to people. I think I try so hard to help people is I want them to need me, as I need something… and when I find someone I think can give me that, my need comes to the fore, as I squish it down for years at a time…

Those who have seen me at my lowest know the truth, as do those who have treated me, every day now, since last November; I have tried to do something for at least one person, whilst looking after myself. I have applied for Christian counseling, so I can get support, but also give back, according to my beliefs and faith….. This way, I hope to keep a healthy balance, more than I have ever done before… it's only the last five or six years I have begun to form real relationships with people. Unfortunately the three most important were with girls I fell in love with, and alas, they didn't feel the same for me, and my neediness got in the way…

The friendships with the men were the other way around and I supported them, I was the strong and silent one but as soon as a women is added to the equation my need causes me to open up to them and I become unable to fend for myself. This is not healthy and can damage both me and them, as it has done before.

For a year or so I made no female friends because I flatly I refused to make any, for fear of the cycle repeating itself, but gradually over the past year I have made some, and I am pleased to say, the balance is holding, it seems I may have finally learned to give and take in equal measure. Those who work with me in a professional capacity seem caught in the past, my old patterns are all to them I think, and if I appear to be even slightly acting in a way I have before they brow beat me with it, saying "you are going back to old patterns of behavior." The simple fact is in order to move forward, sometimes you do use old patterns if you haven't been in that situation before. I am doing voluntary work 20 hours a week, I do not call anyone once a day, let alone the two or three times a day I used to, I don't need to email every day, I don't need to text 20 or thirty times a day anymore.

I can be alone quite easily of late. My patterns may be similar from time to time, but they are not the same. I do not call the crisis team every two weeks these days; I have seen them twice in nine months. I would call that progress, moving on, but thy do not always see that. I think they are scared. I improved dramatically, almost overnight, by myself, and they know they didn't do much to help, but now I struggle, they feel I will slump in the same way, and are powerless to stop it.

I think this is why they are so aggressive at times. They are trying to make me change. But they can't, only I can do that and I try as hard as I humanly can. We all have to do what we can when we can, and if I need other treatment I will accept it, responsibly. For now, I am trying to keep afloat by working hard writing a lot and generally keeping myself busy. Nine times out of ten this approach seems to help me.

But I was talking about relationships. Ok, for my sake and theirs, and to avoid trouble, I wont use real names here… the stories are true, but the names are merely aliases. Firstly there was Gertrude, the first real friend I have had, when I was 19 we met, I hadn't had any real friends before then, not even acquaintances really. Those I met were feared, so I hid. That caused them to taunt me, and bully me. That was really a problem of my own doing, though I couldn't see it, throughout my whole childhood, upto working as a young adult. It's only with hind sight that I can identify these issues. So Gertrude became my friend, then almost like my soul mate. I came to love her, and when she found a partner I tried to kill myself.

Somewhat faulty way of dealing with it, I agree, and I was emotionally ill equipped to deal with this. I was quite frankly immature and still forming emotionally. She told me she loved me, but couldn't see me anymore, it hurt her too much to see me that way, and we never saw each other again, she moved soon after with my best mate Art, and last I heard from him, they split up and went their separate ways with Gertrude settling with another guy. What ever happens I wish them both the best. After this I lost it at work, throwing things around, I fainted, had time off work, saw my doctor and saw a practice therapist who referred me to FDL, and I spent nine months inpatient and 12 months outpatient there.

I left joined remit, a community education project for those with mental health issues and first out a gay youth group at the Llgbc. After a year or two, I met my first real partner, a boy called Dominic, who I came to adore. He was a volunteer at the project, and he wasn't supposed to date with the young people.

Someone found out, and he had to make a choice. He asked me what he should do, and being rather silly and emotional, and romantic and what not, I told him to do what felt right. Just follow his heart and he couldn't go wrong. So he did. He chose the job over me, decided we couldn't be friends either, and I left the group. I never really went back, just the odd time here and there. After that came Rupert who was a year younger but far more experienced in life, with experience in many areas. He was worldly, and wise, or so I thought. It seemed just what a scared young guy needed.

We started going out, till he demanded sex one week in. I wasn't ready, and he threatened to have sex elsewhere. I told him to wait. He asked my permission to do it, I said no. he asked again, and I said do what you want, but don't expect me to go out if you sleep around. I'm just not ready yet, not a common attitude with a young guy I admit, but I am much more sensitive than your average 26 year old fella, I think. Either way that is what happened and he went and got his end away, and so we split up.

I emotionally unstable and quickly fell in with Reginald who said for months he had liked me, and wanted to go out, but as soon as he was ready to act, I went out with Rupert. He told me stuff about him, and it made me glad we had split. Reginald turned out to be somewhat dangerous, having served time in jail for hacking, at least that's what he told me at the time. He was on curfew at a hostel and if he broke it he was instantly on recall back to jail.

I accepted this until the day he used his phone to call for a taxi home. A few days' later plain clothes police turned up at my door asking after him. They dealt with me at home, and then came to see me at my supported housing project, after I agreed to talk with them. It turned out sweet Reg wasn't a hacker, never had been. He was wanted coz he had broken curfew and was on a runner from the police. They suspected him being involved in the case of a small girl. As you can imagine this was horrifying to me and I started feeling suicidal and self harming. Happily, as soon as the truth became known, and they knew I didn't know any more than the fact he was in Leeds they went after him. I have simplified this somewhat, as it would take ten pages or more to go into depth, lets just say that was the worst three months or so I had ever had up to that point.

They came round a few more times over a few months, told me they had him, and that was the last I heard. I knew a mate of mine had helped them with the inquiry too, and that's all I ever knew. I think he is still in jail on a five year sentence, or so the police told me two years ago… That was the last time I went out with anyone. Two years later I am single, still a virgin and still unsure of what a real relationship feels like. For those smart arse's who say "you haven't lived, you can't talk because you haven't even had a lasting relationship. You're so inexperienced, pampered and naive"

I say, say that without knowing a person and you become victim of stereotypical thinking and you are at risk of being labeled yourself an insensitive, un-empathetic emotionally retarded idiot, by me, if no-one else.

I have a huge amount of life experience, I have survived over ten years of depression self harm, a collected four years of therapy, seven crisis tem admissions, four inpatient admissions in the Bradgate unit, two careers, 12 qualifications, many, many hors of voluntary work, three years working 12 hour shifts at night, three homes, many, many people in my life. When it comes to self awareness, I think I'm pretty good. When it comes to general experiences mine rival most peoples I think, newspaper interviews, videos on video nation, a short video or two for the educational services, articles in national magazines and papers, two sci-fi comedy manuscripts being prepared for sending to a publisher…..

Yeah, I think I have done quite a bit. Please do not think me arrogant, I'm merely saying I have done stuff, seen stuff. I'm no better than anyone else, but I also won't allow others to sneer at me. They have no right, the same way as I have no right to do that to anyone either. We are all the same really I think. Maybe it is only environment that causes us to react differently. It is what we do, not what we think that makes us who we are. Two people could be abused as children, one becomes a killer, and one becomes a teacher. Similar experiences, different actions. I really do believe that. It's down to your make up, your heart condition that makes you who you are. We can modify ourselves to a certain extent, learn new coping mechanisms, but we cannot remake our heart and souls.

But I am wavering off topic, becoming obsessed by detail. After this, there was Kate and Clare, the two most beautiful people there have ever been in my life, and true to past form, they both completed me, and devastated me at the same time.

This time around the blame was not mine alone, although I significantly endangered the later relationship with Clare. This was a nightmare than I am only starting to emerge from. It hurts to discuss it, it hurts to think on it, and though it's been almost a year since we spoke, it's still a little too raw to deal with easily. So I shall start with Kate. Even though it was hard at the time, it was nothing to compare with what was to come later. I think it is true what doesn't kill you makes you stronger. It's a good saying is that? What they don't tell you is, you often wish it had killed you.

I first met Clare when we were in FDL together, we became friends, and things were going well till I saw her crying and I went to speak to her, and she was crying, so I naturally put my hand on her shoulder to offer support. That was silly, as I didn't yet realize people who have suffered greatly value their own space. I learnt this lesson quickly, but at that time I was quite unawares. She screamed that I reminded her of her rapist, and screamed for me to leave her, so the other girls there asked me to go with them, coz she was upset. Was mortified, but I did. Then Clare said In a meeting she couldn't deal with me, so I let her be. Having me talked about that way was so hard; it was in therapy for days after that. Then she decided to sit next to me, and a guy called philbert said she wasn't being fair to me, and I had feelings too…. And nobody seemed to recognize this. Well after this they did, and she ran away at 3 in the morning up the main road in her pajamas, and she was sectioned again.

I met her three years later, and we became friends again. She came along to a plus-group meeting where we were preparing our bits and pieces to speak to some nurses. We started speaking; although neither of us really let on we remembered the others. We started speaking about fave bands, which was the very first conversation we had had, so we repeated it three years later, and slowly we became best friends, and for a couple of years it was wonderful, we were study buddies, both doing OU at the time, training mates, we both trained together, we spent lots of time together, it got so we were speaking at least once a night, more often twice at least, and we saw each other at least twice a week socially.

That's when I started to become compulsive and addicted to her, and old patterns came to the fore once again. Things started to go wrong, as I needed her more and more. I can remember when this reached its peak, before I started my inevitable slide downwards, and the relationship imploded and ended. I was at a Plus Group meeting when I received a call from the police saying I had been broken into, and I freaked out, thinking it was Reginald back again to torment me, or one of his dodgy mates. I thought he knew I had grassed him up, and had sent the good squad after me. I went home, and the lock was smashed in. my neighbor had found my door open apparently, I found later, and went in to look around, coz he knew I had mental health problems and was worried I may have topped myself.

I hadn't of course, though I had come close to it many times both before, and afterwards. He had shut the door, and reported me missing to the police... they had made a call, and I came home... to find the door smashed in, by the police who were looking for evidence, and to double check things. I had already told them I was alright, but when I got home the sight of my papers everywhere freaked me so badly Clare took me to her house... I ended up staying there for four days or so, and it was then that the obsessiveness reached its peak. I felt safer than I had ever been before, and I started to see her as my savior. I put her on a pedestal I was rather emotionally immature, and always had found her remarkably wonderful. She is just so amazing a person you fall for her. And this of course made things hard for me.

I started asking to stop at her house and she kept saying no, coz we both knew we were getting too close.. From that point I called her every night for nearly two years, she was who I went to if I had problems, she became my counselor even though I had never intended that to happen. We weren't really friends anymore, but we loved each other that way.... But she was taking care of me, more and more. It was unfair on her, it was my fault, I was being selfish, but I was psychotic, suicidal, out of control, and I couldn't help it. I started shouting a lot at her, which was bloody stupid, I was a git. I always apologized, but I was losing control, and when I started smashing things whilst talking to her on the phone, it really strained the friendship. She said we needed to build trust back up, she was vulnerable, and I apologized...

But I kept on doing what I was doing and inevitably it went badly wrong, we both said awful things and to date we have spoken once in a year, swapped a few texts and three or four emails, and that's it…. In a year.

We went out that night, me her and her partner… lets call him jock. (He will hate being called jock!!! He is a cool bloke.) she had told a mate of hours she loved me, we went on to another pub, she drank loads, as did her bloke, I drank a bit, started to disassociate, seeing weird colors and shapes, couldn't make sense of sounds or smells and couldn't talk, was sobbing with my head on the table for over an hour. She didn't once ask me if I was ok, but I know she was talking about stuff that upset her, things she was struggling with… not sure what, coz I was so psychotically ill that night, I ran out into the path of a taxi, but realized I needed help, but couldn't go back in there, it freaked me so much so I texted and rang and rang.

She wouldn't answer so I left a message asking why she was doing this I explained the situation said I was suicidal and needed help. She sent jock out, who told me to chill forget it and come drink more. He said Clare couldn't help me if I didn't explain. So I tried, and I cried and clenched my fists. That set her off and she said she didn't care. I said I was suicidal and she said she didn't care. That hurt me so, so, so badly. So I told her to get fucked and ran away. I rang her loads to give apologies and was still angry so told her how much she hurt me, and that was it. We never really spoke again.

She emailed and told me how she had suddenly realized I had never been a friend to her and I hadn't ever treated her with respect. This sobered me and I realized just how much I must have wounded her, and I had never been there for her, and never been a friend. I apologies and asked her to forgive me. She said the love was still there but we had to rebuild foundations slowly before we got to where we were before. But neither of us really wanted that. I told her she saying she didn't care if I killed myself had wounded me so badly I lost it and reacted so badly, and I was out of order but so had her saying that. But I was more worried for her now, and I just wanted to forget it and do whatever she wanted me to do, to keep her friendship and make it upto her. Over the months she moved on, so did I getting voluntary work and stuff and things have just faded? I still care for her deeply and would love to forge a proper friendship over time, but I'm not sure if that's possible.

She runs a support forum online I have always used since she told me about it in early 2004, and have recently left that coz it was too painful to see her reply to my posts, knowing she cared, but wouldn't see or speak to me anytime soon. So I decided to make a clean break, and enable us to rebuild again afresh. That decision is a painful one, as I have made many friends on the forum and feel that I have helped quite a lot of folk. They say this is true, so I believe them. I hope this in part makes up for my shitty behavior in the past. All I can do is continue to change, and in a year I have made so much progress. I can't undo the past; only continue to act as I do in the future.

Jock has always been a sound guy, caring for me even though I acted badly and hurt the one he loved. He frequently tired to help whilst setting boundaries, and

I will always respect him and care for him. He is a true gent, gentle and strong, and suffering greatly himself. Or at least he was a year ago. I will never forget such an amazing soul. The pair of them are amazing people. No matter what happened, I will always treasure the fact they were in my life, and I had friends like them. I don't think I was worthy, I hope to be again one day… everything that has occurred to this point has helped mature me, round me, make me a better person, and I think I'm probably a better friend these days. I know I think much deeper, am aware of people's emotions more, pick up on micro movements and body language. My spider senses tingle. God, I loved Spiderman as a kid. That's irrelevant right now 'I'm sure.

So to recap, I feel extremely ashamed and humbled by my responses in the past, I have been a bit of a jerk, not through any nastiness or vindictiveness, but merely through inadaptability, immaturity, loss of control, fear, lust and longing, mental illness, and a lack of empathy or thought of others. When you are suicidal and so in need of help, your human caring goes out the window, you switch to survival mode and you do anything to get by. Even if that is damaging wounding and hurting others. It's awful, selfish, bad, but you can't always help it. All you can do is work on minimizing the damage, separate for a while and try to learn from your mistakes.

 I feel I have done that, my partners and patterns have over time, have changed, I am much more balanced, I will seek help from friends, but I will get the main support from professionals. I intend this to be from Christian counseling, so my faith is central to my growth...

It will help me be a better follower of Christ, less selfish, more empathic, but also get me the help I need, focusing around the love of god, and his grace compassion and the knowledge I am one of his children. That he is my father. I am attempting to do this whilst helping others as much as I can, but making sure I look after myself. This is a more humanistic way of doing things I feel. In this way I have united both sides of me. as I have already stated, I do know that I have a seriously problematic way of getting to know a person, but knowledge is power and having an awareness of a problem makes it so much easier to work to find a solution, and that's what I am doing right now.

Trying to rebuild the foundations of my life, work on my rough edges, whilst doing everything to help those who need me, safeguarding both of us, so that we both get what we need. Looking back I can see where I went wrong, every time, but the experience I have, the urge to make amends, and to live a more balanced and selfless life, is something I am actually so grateful for. I think the saying is true.

What doesn't kill you does make you stronger, though you wish you hadn't survived the learning for quite a time afterward. I have a heavy heart, but it's a good one, and that must count for something surely? I have asked for forgiveness from Clare and others I may have hurt, most have given it, Clare has I think, in so many words, but more importantly I have asked it of god, and meant it, I have repented, and I repent everyday. I struggle to forgive myself, but if god has then I should. I guess it's a case of "by the grace of god go I".

There is so much stress in my life right now that I have neglected my relationship with god, and this is not helping me, and I know I need to sort it out, and talk to god in prayer and spend time building my personal relationship with him, getting to know him through his word, worship, prayer and private time just talking to him. So whilst I have done wrong in my life, I have tried to make it better myself, and when that failed, prayed to god to help mend fences and repair and heal those who I have harmed by my inadequate ways. So, I have previously said I have apologised in full both to them and more importantly to god. I have asked for forgiveness, and have been forgiven. It therefore is my hope that 2006 is a clean slate for me.

I realise now, I have to face my demons, my fears, insecurities, anxieties that sprung from the way I grew up, what happened. Only by doing so can I move on, and live a relatively healthy life. This is my ultimate goal. To be happy, and to make others happy in the process, those I love and cherish. I can do this only through the grace of god, knowing he loves me and forgives me. I think it's only through the Holy Spirit that I can truly be renewed. Its only when god makes everyone perfect that suffering will truly leave the world, but until then I need to pray, and to take counsel.

I guess what I have trying to get at upto now, is that I have horrendous symptoms; I suffer mental distress, but am not mentally ill. I truly believe this. My experiences of society, make me react a certain way, which can be shitty and not so good, but society is the crazy thing, not the individual, some are just more sensitive to the madness than others.

I would like to share my thoughts with you about mental health, society, and the links between them. Let's look at what mental illness is, let me start off by saying I have a so called "personality Disorder" which Indicates my whole personality is flawed, that it doesn't work right, that I don't fit in with society.

It kind of makes me think the Doctors think that I cannot function in this order of things. This is not true and over the past few months I have proven this one. Ok it is hard for me to function, but I do and I can. Ok. I am not the only one. There are hundreds, if not millions of us, all with assorted "illnesses and disorders." Are you with me so far? Great. That is excellent. Right.

I don't think that it's us with the flaw. We are involved in a process of change, we are changing and growing, learning more, changing so that we no longer fit within the box, we in the western world are changing. The new generations are becoming more spiritually and mentally aware. Thinkers, poets and artists are emerging again. There are true sensitives who don't buy in to traditional values. It seems we are no longer content to act as we are taught, no longer content to believe in a society that doesn't work at all well. Not able to fit in with "modern society" no sense of pride in our nations, unable to hold down a nine-to-five existence, the job, the family, etc. I still see things that make me see red, and I am not a very good Christian in my attitudes at time. I still sometimes swear, curse, and am rude. I try not to be, but there are some things that seriously stretch me. This is because there are people who do not belong in this society the way it is. They cannot function within it, they are like an infection rejected by an antibody.

I am one of those I feel. It's because this current regime is a disease, and we are the antibodies. Its false, empty, it does not mean anything. More and more of us are thinking, "What is the point of this life? Is this existence worth it, as the world is?" and we answer no. So then we ask' "so what am I here for, what is my purpose?"

That is Simple. We are here to change it. But we don't realise it, because we are brainwashed by this society from birth. But we must change it. If we are to bring the Kingdom of god, we must work at improving things. But we don't do we? I think I know why this is. We are conditioned to earn money, eat, sleep, and repeat the cycle all over again, this is an awful and false existence. And on some level, we are aware of that. Society urges us to dress the same, think the same, have the same haircut, and comply. And we cannot, because we simply are not made that way.

In my view, and this is only from my view point, this causes us to fear we are going insane. We feel suicidal, loosing our sense of identity, but does this mean we are mentally ill? I doubt it. Is there truly such a thing as mental illness? Society says so, the professionals, the psychiatrists, the psychotherapists, councillors and doctors. What is evident is that many people do not fit in with the moral majority. And who labels this minority? The Majority of Society.

They have come up with a whole plethora of mental illnesses, descriptions, and diagnosis to explain away our differences, explaining why we don't fit in with the rest of society. I have a different view. We are not mentally ill at all. I think what they describe as "mental illness" is a sane response to an insane world.

Those who are sensitive, poets, artists, those who think outside of the box, those that cannot accept this world, they are the ones who become "mentally ill". They are so labelled because they cannot exist in a society that is so chaotic and false. They do not fit in with a world which is going to hell in a hand basket.

What is this "society?" When you look at it, we have world leaders we cannot trust, making war for oil, and profit, and because we have too many treaties and agreements, to satisfy their need for aggression. Who wins? Not the soldiers. Not the normal citizens. Those at the top, that's who. Greed and corruption, these have been the watchwords. Society is stale, and it's falling apart at the seams. We live in a time where our politicians are untrustworthy, where they act for their own interests, not for us. We live in a world where the drug dealers, the murderers, the assassins, they are on top and in control.

We live in an insane world where people starve in one part of the world, and where others get fat and rich, controlling everybody else. Look at us here in England, where our young men are sent out to war to fight for our governments and our country, because "our leaders" decide it's necessary. I can't belong to such an insane society. I would rather be on the outside, an exile than participate in such a vile deception.

It's only so that we are in control, and not controlled, because it's a dog eat dog society where it's either control or be controlled, destroy, or be destroyed. But why live this way? It does not have to be this way. We can decide to change. But we will not.

Because one side or the other wants what the other has, want to control them, and so millions die on both sides. Look at all this bullshit. The worlds fucked up. Look around you. It's true. Is this a safe world and do you feel you fit in with it? I don't. So I ask again, what is a mental illness? If there is such a thing, it's a global one, all of society is "mentally ill" and we don't belong within it. It's a symptom of a deeper disease, a dysfunctional world. Maybe it has always been his way, but I believe its getting worse.

No bloody wonder some of us exhibit strange and disturbing symptoms! I am not putting down sufferers of these symptoms, I know they are real, the pain, the distress, the anxiety and fear, I know all these are real. Some here voices, some self-harm, some have delusions and hallucinations, and to those suffering them, they are absolutely real, I am not disputing that, I am saying it does not make us mentally ill. I am not denying the fact we feel ill or unwell, because we do, and that's that, I am merely stating my opinion that it's because we are sensitive to the world around us and the chaos it contains,

And that we are not able to cope with it precisely because we are not unwell! The world is, and we can see it for what it is, pure madness. On some gut instinctive level, we all know its wrong and it does not work. Some have a clearer view, understand the politics, and motivations, some just have a muddy feel something is wrong. It's because society is wrong! Therefore, there is no such thing as "Mental illness" just varying degrees of ability to work within a society that is fundamentally flawed. Is a matter of spirituality, conscience and personality?

I am not saying that modern methods cannot help us, for instance medication, and counselling can help in the right context. I don't believe psychotherapy works because its based around helping you to fit into today's society, which you cannot do, but if the professionals realised this, and worked at changing society, Then psychotherapy could perhaps work, as the society it was working to integrate us into would be a working and healthy one, one which would cherish our fundamental character traits.

There are already mechanisms in place and people who want to change are society, but they are all disparate, separate, coming at it from different view points and directions. That is the way it is now. But if they were all brought together, if every faction worked at the same goal, from those different directions, but co-ordinated, then it is entirely possible. For instance, you have the environmentalists, who want to save the environment, green peace who wants to save species. There is the organisation CND who are against nuclear, and chemical war, and power.

There are aid groups who provide medical aid as well as food. There are mental health activists who want to change the system, anti-dictator-groups etc, amnesty international, and countless others. If these all somehow, could see the bigger picture, see themselves as pieces to the same puzzle, we could change this world, and unite behind the same banner: I hope that within my life time we can all rely on harmony and peace for all, where physical and emotional sufferings are drastically reduced.

I feel this is the only way world peace, a healthy and green world, true scientific discovery, and a united human race, where mental illness does not exist, can come into being. So let's recap. Let's look at my semi-coherent ramblings and try to make sense of them. In order for this to happen we have to understand ourselves. Understand ourselves in context of not having a "mental illness" but being fundamentally unable to integrate into a society, which is un-untreatable! We are evolving as a species, with the new generations thinking and feeling different to those that came before.

Because of that there is bound to be birthing pains, problems that are caused by a race struggling to reinvent itself from the bottom up, and it manifests itself as so called "mental illness" And so I believe it is not wrong to be the way we are, its just a symptom, and it can be reduced, the symptoms will go when the problem is solved, and that problem is our society And the way we treat each other.

I am not some fanatic who says down with society, I don't want anarchy, for who would benefit from that? But I would a better society where we are al equal. I may sound like I am repeating myself but I feel this point is very important, and must be understood by all of us if a real change is to be made.

Now I don't think I am clever and some super-brain, certainly not. There are better minds than mine looking at this problem. I am aware that many others have come to this conclusion/ I am sure, this is the case because if I have, then others must've, but if more of us talk about this, it makes it real.

And society must then look at it and change, it may take hundreds of years, but it will happen. I firmly believe this. It will, because if it doesn't, we will destroy ourselves. It's us, the ordinary folk the little people who need to put pressure on our governments to make a changed. And we are doing, things are changing, but it needs to happen sooner, more voices need to be added to the Chorus. At this point, I feel I must add that this part of "Littleboylost" is the product of thoughts that I have been having on and off for the past three or so years, and of a couple of drunken conversations I had with friends on New Years Eve 2003, in Leicester. So it is apt that on New years day 2005 two years later these thoughts come to fruition only to be published within this book. The conversations were primarily about my searching for a point to existence.

Existentialism came up, as my friends are existentialists, and they were talking about how life is absurd has no meaning, and me not being able to except there isn't a point to existence. That there is not some purpose, and also about how the world is fucked up, stale and hostile, with war and corruption rife. We talked about philosophy and our symptoms, about seeking some deep hidden truth, extensionalism and this started off the process again within my mind, of the thoughts which came together as the work you read here. I was on an acute ward a couple of years or so ago now, and I really saw for the first time just how upset and confused people can get.

And I saw just how "ill" people can be, and I thought about how the system allows this, without truly helping them. And during this time I thought about my own experience of psychotherapy, within a Leicestershire. The first lot I had.

– based at a therapeutic community, which was based on how we behave, how we present ourselves focusing on our own guilt, Anger and how we can address these to grow in citizenship, working on your issues, so that you could fit in with society. Society is the problem if you ask me...

By now, we see this is flawed, and it made me consider what changes were necessary in order to prevent the symptoms we exhibit. It's a bit of a tough one that, and essentially a question of philosophy and the way we view the world. I am becoming more and more certain of how I see things and I am certain that this is the truth of it. Of course I realise others will disagree, be hurt or angered by what I have to say, but its there. It is what I firmly believe. It helps this is all mentioned in the bible. Nations turning on nations etc, etc.

In the meantime, I Accept that in the past I have I needed help, hospital Admissions, and for some I know medication and suchlike can help, as I have previously said, but it's not a cure. The only way to stop all this is for society to change. It's a matter of personal responsibility, I feel. Before I close now, and go on off again, to think and write some more,
I feel I need to say, Thank-you to you those who have been my friends, the ones who made me think this way, I already owe you a lot. I owe you for so many Reasons. Mostly because you helped pull me back from the brink, so to speak, but you also helped me to make up my mind, and write this.

Probably wouldn't have, without you stimulating me. So thanks guys, thanks a lot. You know who you are! Also I have been influenced and inspired by the book "spiritual emergency" which was contributed to by various authors, and by the book "indigo child". There are so many to mention and I have not the space to even try. But I feel I should mention also the books "the peaceful warrior" and "the life you were born to live" by Dan Millan". William Boroughs and "Naked lunch" which, I have to say – disturbed, confused and inspired me, in a roundabout way as well.

This kind of brings me full circle, back to now, how I am feeling now, about my place in the grand scheme of things. It brings me back to how I feel, how lonely and soulless, dead, I feel at times. Wondering where I belong. What I want from life. I think that finally, after many false starts, I am on my way; I have started my journey towards recovery. Now recovery is a concept banded about in many mental health circles, it's become clichéd' and some don't believe in it any more, but I do.

I think Recovery will take me the rest of my life, as it's not all plain sailing, but deciding I want to help myself. Deciding that I want to take responsibility for myself, and pull myself up, get help, and get on with life – that's the first step. The beginning steps to Recovery to me are quite simple. When I no longer sit there, Mentally screaming please help me, and not getting to the stage, when you would do anything to be able to make the memories lurking at the back of your mind like shadowy demons to go away. That is Recovery. When the whispers of those who were meant to protect you no longer sound like shouts in your mind, when they no longer have power over you; this is recovery, at least to me.

To me recovery is getting back to a stage in my life, where I knew without a shadow of a doubt that I was going to get through today, and tomorrow would come and it was all good, it was fine. Recovery would be when there was no mind numbing terror, no paranoia that as soon as I was out of ear shot people would laugh at me, think I was stupid. I had no fear of being physically attacked, walking out of my home down to the shops didn't paralyse me, I didn't lie in bed shaking for hours afterwards.

That to me would be recovery – an ability to lead my life, as I want without having to contend with voices, paranoia, panic attacks or anything of that nature. I am no longer sure of whom I am. Sure, on my birth certificate it states, "Adam pick born 24/07/1979", but these are just words. I have no real sense of ME at all. It is coming back some, wanting to be an ambulance technician, my ethics, my morals, and stuff. Its coming back slowly. But I am not as certain as I used to be of who I was.

I did once; I had no questions about that. I remember how it felt. I was strong and calm, sure of myself, my likes, desires, needs, all that stuff. I had clear goals. I don't any longer. I cannot honestly tell you what I am going to be doing next week, because the suicidal thoughts do sometimes get so bad at the moment I can barely comprehend being here tomorrow. I think recovery for me, is purely being able to see my way clear to the end of the week, without having flashes of killing myself, or sudden urges to burn my arm with my iron, etc. that is recovery.

I don't want to earn millions, have a successful career even. I no longer want to be a web designer or a pc engineer; I just want to be free of this emotional pain I feel. I want not to feel like screaming, because it hurts that much.Recovery to me is accepting the events of my childhood, rape, physical and mental abuse, and getting away from the memories. Getting to a stage in my own life, where the memories don't make me feel I am about to collapse to me knees and vomit. At the moment I cannot do this. I get so panicky it's like people are not speaking English to me, even when they are. My balance goes completely, colours shift, I feel faint, its like people are ghostly, not there.

I then feel like I will vomit, and I sit, or lie and I shiver. I just lie there and shiver, my heart beating so fast and so hard, it feels like it is going to burst out of my chest, and lay on the floor, quivering.When I no longer go through this, week in week out, no panic, no flashes of anger so intense I cannot think, no panic so painful I cannot make sense of the world, when this no longer affects me, then I will have considered myself to have recovered.

I wrote this poem when I was trying to decide whether or not to live or die. I decided I did not want to live the way I was any longer, so I had to make a choice, die, or recover. If I died, there would be no pain, to me, but it would hurt others, but if I lived and recovered, I would be happy and so would those I loved. And because I am a Christian Death by suicide has become abhorrent to me anyhow, just as a life in pain is also. Quite A little paradox there.So this poem was my asking the question – what should I do? Nobody answered… and then, I answered myself. So here it is – "A question"

A Question.

CAN I throw it all away? Just rip it up,
And throw it all away.
Delve into madness,
And drown in this dark,
And velvety sea.

To resurface again one day,
To take back what is mine, and take it away,
 from them, the well ones,
the keepers of my hope.

A question.

That's all this is, a plaintive cry,
A scream into the night,
A tortured soul,
Who is dying slowly?

A question.

 SHOULD I throw it away?
 Give up on this,
The false hope of a fool,
And resign myself,
 to the sweet nectar which is death?
A question. Yes,
Just that,

A question.
I ask it,
But nobody deems fit to answer.

And so I decided to live.

It's not that simple however. I have decided to live yes, but more than that, I decided to take that step and recover. It hasn't been plain sailing, by any means, but I have started down that path, at last.

And as narrow, and windy as it is, with thorns covering my path, and strange beasts living in the shadows, I am making my way. I am Persevering. But once I had made that decision to do so, I felt remorse and sorrow, because deciding to live is very hard, and giving up on the easy option is not so easy.

In this poem, I asked why would those who helped me, why had they done so. Why did they feel I deserved to live? It was a form of closure for me also. So here it is "Life not worth Living"

Life not worth living.

Why would you want to?
 You save a life not worth saving?
When all that life can feel'
 Is that deathly craving?
I wanted to die, but I did not,
Trying now to live,
But don't know how,
Great Scott.

You came, and you comforted,
And you gave me the best of you,
God' it was appreciated,
But what made you bother?
What do I mean to you?
It would've been so easy to let it all
Go.

Why didn't I? Oh fuck.

Why didn't I?
Suicide,
Such I pretty word.

Why would you want to?
You save a life not worth saving?

When all that life can feel'
Is that deathly Craving?
I wanted to die, but I did not,
Trying now to live,
But don't know how, great Scott.

When I was sitting there, in that ward,
 I felt so safe and life was something to regain and grasp,
 But now I am home again,
 And slowly I start to fall,
 And suicide, oh how it calls,
 Before just a word,
 Now it seems to be my destiny.

Why didn't I Oh bollocks?
Why didn't I?
Suicide,
Such a pretty thought.

You came, and you comforted,
And you gave me toe best of you,
God' it was appreciated,
But what made you bother?
What do I mean to you?
Before you came,
It was so easy to let it go.

Now that door is closed to me forever.
And I look forward in quiet
Hope.

Once I had decided to live and recover, I was able to see how friends had pulled me through, especially my then closest friend. I have lost her because of my erratic behaviour when I was fighting to live. But she saved my life. She really did, back then. Without that firm, but gentle guiding hand I would have given up. This poem was I guess, my way of mourning and easy way out, and thanking those who cared for me at the same time. It was a way of saying good bye to easy ways out, a memo to myself, that from hereon in, I would do nothing short of my best, to get a life, and more importantly, keep it.

To Recover to me equates to freedom. Freedom of a malicious subconscious. and conspicuous ever-present pain. I just want to be able to do the simple things in life that every one takes for granted. When I can live the life I want, without constant terror, I will then be firmly on the way to recovery, and part of that, I feel, is finding a partner, a love, someone who touches me deep inside.

I admit it. At this point, I must come clean, and state that which is foremost on my mind. I must speak a very simple truth. I want only to be loved. Pathetic that, isn't it, eh? The pain that I feel, its funny, I didn't realise pain could be sweet, cloying, like honey. I didn't realise it could be a dull throb, as well as an intense teeth-pulling-agony. I have experienced both. The need to be loved is a constant throb, which rises in pitch to a sharp pain, and then drops, into background noise, once again.

But it is there, always, consistently, there. It's a good hurt, sometimes, welcome, perhaps it's because it's been a constant companion, since childhood? Or perhaps it's because deep down, I feel I deserve to feel this way, and am excepting of my fate? It matters little. Quite simply, I want to not be alone any more, I want to move on, and take the next step, to find me lost half, my soul mate. I am quite spiritual in my outlook, I always have been. Do not confuse this with religious thinking. That is very new to me. I am now religious, but I have always been spiritual. And I feel pulled, guided, moved, to find some-one…

Find someone who wants to be my eternal love. The person who wants to be my eternal companion. I am some what of a romantic, and I believe there is someone for everyone out there, the trick is in finding them, I guess. I need love. And need it fast! As do we all, for sure. I am ready to give up the life of a bachelor, and to become one of two.

CHAPTER EIGHT

Alone, I am incomplete, half a whole, or perhaps merely a quarter of the being, I could be, the man I should be. Perhaps, I need a mate, or more likely I need a soul mate, A fusion of spiritual and carnal needs that means you have found the one who will complete you. I am missing my other half, the ying to my yang, the salve to calm my fire, the cool caress that soothes all fears.

The backbone that holds me, the love that redeems me. And then delivers me reborn, into the world anew, like the phoenix from the flames, the abandoned soul welcomed back into the caring embrace of those who had forsaken me. Renewed, complete, and whole, body and soul.

I hunger for that sense of completeness, I long for the cessation of this remorseless drive to be more than I, and I seek Redemption, a deliverance from this travesty that is my life. I seek togetherness that will be mine for eternity; I seek the connection, the sharing of souls, and the pure bond which only a lover could impart to me. The thing which friendship is only a pale imitation of. I seek the fusion of body and mind, the merging of my soul with that of another.

Nirvana to me is the connection between spirits, minds, and souls. The joy of starting a sentence only to have it completed by your other half. That pure joy of having a thought, only to find it mirrored in the heart of your loved one. The pure elation of your katra being joined to that of one possessing endless compassion, love and wisdom, opened to you, and you alone.

Heaven and hell are states of mind; hell is to be without love. Hell is to be unaware of that eternal bond, or indeed to have had it, and have it ripped away, tore from your being, the shock of disconnection. The removal of the other from your heart, and your mind, to know the pure joy of that scared bond was no longer present in your beloved's soul. That is the true meaning of hell. All else can be endured.

Heaven is the presence of that holiest of holy' pure unadulterated love. And that is the essence of the constant acceptance, compassion, knowing that you are a part of another's heart, mind, and soul. That, you are with that person eternally, in their heart, mind, and soul, that you are only a thought away from them, and they you. Knowing that they cherish you, and you belong with them, that you will be together always, side by side. That is heaven.

But both of these experiences are transitory, and it remains to be seen which one is predominant, which one lasts for longer. To see which will imprint upon our souls. And change us for ever. Which one will influence us as we step from the present into the future, and forever change our lives? Will I be saved, or will I be lost? The loneliness' is killing me, dissolving me from within, like a powerful poison. Or perhaps an even stronger acid that is slowly dissolving my insides my spirit and my soul.

Indeed, the very things that make me Adam, they are fading. They are atrophying, fading, shrivelling and dying. The guilt, the Anger, the Shame, the roaring frustration and sense of injustice are consuming the core, the real me. I am slowly being undone. I am being undone by myself and by my pain and by my conscience and by a thousand factors. I am fragmentary, a thousand shards, containing a tiny portion of that which I could be. Together they form a whole, but they are not combined, not together, I do not think I have been whole since my earliest days. I am waiting for someone, somebody to help me heal myself, and reunite each of my solitary fragments, into one whole pane of glass.

One Gloriously complete mirror with which to shine my light outwards, becoming the person I have always longed to be. But I am finding becoming the person I should be particularly difficult. At the moment I am physically rather unwell. I have not mentioned this upto this point, as I felt there were far more important topics for me to raise, but my health is not good, and I feel weaker every day that passes. Some days are good ones, but others not so. As I write this chapter it is march the fifth, 2006, and I have been suffering blackouts since December last year. I have had to my count roughly 17 or 18 losses of consciousness in that time. I have been in hospital five times during this period, four of them overnight and the second from last for nine days, as I was very ill.

The time before that, my blood pressure was 186, and the emergency doctor who came to see me rushed me straight into the LRI onto ward sixteen for assessment and treatment. Since then, I have had an EEG, the tracing of the brainwaves, a CT scan of my brain, an X-ray of my body, and ECG heart trace, a 24 hour ECG heart trace, numerous blood tests, and the doctors still aren't sure what is occurring. I am still waiting to hear about this last battery of tests, the EEG and ECG, and the situation has become more aggravated of late as I have recently been in hospital again overnight because I had 4 blackouts in one hour on the same day of late, luckily thy were all witnessed else I would not have known about them, and so couldn't tell the doctors. It may be I have had many more than I remember if this latest event is more common place than we realise.

Either way it is upsetting and scary. I have blacked out in my bath alone, waking only to find that the water is seeping over my mouth. I bolted awake, nearly smashing my head on the wall behind me, having a panic attack crying out loud, and stumbling out of the bath, slipping on the floor and scaring myself silly. I have slipped twice at work on the stairs, and fell bodily down my own due to lost balance and concentration. The doctors have referred me to the falls clinic which I must attend as well as the neurology and general clinics until they know what is wrong with me.

At least the time I spent in hospital roused my creative spirit somewhat. I met a very interesting guy who I shall call "Cedric". He was most peculiar, and I rather liked him. I have written this short piece to commemorate or time together, side by side, in the hospital of certain doom. (Commonly known as the general hospital, Leicester.)

So here it is... Hope you enjoy reading it, as much as I enjoyed writing it.

"Cedric, don't poke the patients"

Hospitals are never the most enjoyable of places, and they are usually hellishly boring, but at least this time around, my time there was interesting. Well, at least for the first night or so. I was wheeled onto the EMU ward of the general hospital, Leicester after a blackout which resulted in me landing on my head, with my legs up on my chair, one arm under my desk and the other on my printer on the floor, behind my desk (trust me, you had to have seen it, to believe it, I imagine it was quite amusing. I don't know, I was unconscious at the time.)

About five in the morning, and I promptly fell asleep after the poking and prodding had ended.

No sooner had I fled consciousness with great glee, hoping never to return, than I felt this presence hovering over me, and being half unconscious, unable to move, sick, dizzy and mentally malfunctioning, I assumed it was god. Opening my eyes I discovered this wasn't the case at all. It was some old guy, with his lips about a millimeter from my nose. Blinking in surprise, I could only ask "Are you lost, mate? Or am I your type or something?" hey, it was short notice, and I had to come up with something.

"You're in my bed". That was his only reply. Now, I knew my sense of reality wasn't exactly secure, but I was fairly sure this dude was either nuts, or plainly wrong. Therefore I had no problem with stating the facts as I knew them "nah. Im so not in your bed mate." I was hoping that was the end of it. Yeah right, like life is that easy.

"How do you know it's not my bed" he asked in a triumphant way. Looking at him like he had shat on the ward floor, I explained as gently as I could (which wasn't very gently, actually) "I know it's my bed coz I was asleep in it when they wheeled me onto the ward. You weren't in it then, so I know its mine. Ok?"

He looked at me for a long moment, obviously deciding not to pursue the matter, nodded, and slouched away, leaving a smell like rotting cabbage behind him. I shook my head, doubting my sanity, and tried to think of pleasant thoughts. After a time I calmed somewhat.

Feeling I had handled this one rather well, I smiled benignly and closed my eyes, promptly leaving the land of the awake for a place much more to my liking. Then the next thing I know, I felt like a vulture was pecking its way into my abdomen. I let out a kind of strangled yell, opened one eye, to find this old guy looming over me once again, with his finger's where they should not have been. It was somewhat disconcerting I am sure you can see. Footsteps resounded as a nurse came on over, quick as Lightening. There was a foreboding silence. And then the nurse came out with it. I couldn't believe my ears. It was like a bleeding comedy sketch: "Cedric don't poke the patients" with that she departed in a cloud of cheap perfume, clearly feeling her work ere was done.

I closed my eyes with the pain of it all. How bloody ironic. Or moronic, depends on your point of view. Either way, I wasn't impressed. "You having fun, or what?" I asked him, in a rather grouchy way. He just mumbled in reply as he shuffled off back to his bed. And that's where he stayed. This is rather lucky for him. Because by this point, I was willing to bodily hang him out of an open window. Not especially Christian I know, but I wasn't feeling too well. Come on; give a boy a break, yeah?"

All joking aside, it was quite a scary time for me, the nine days felt like they were 90. I began to doubt I would ever leave. The past three weeks I find I am extremely physically weak, so tired by the time I leave my voluntary job I am almost falling over on the bus, crawling up the stairs and literally collapsing into bed before I can pull my clothes off. I often awake to find myself clothed. I am unconscious before six pm, sometimes as early as 5pm and I am sick of it.

This is every night, by 12 or one I feel so ill and unwell, I get so dizzy all day, have these blackouts, and sleep most of the weekend, cant move in the morning when I wake, my muscles wont respond for a an hour or two….

This is seriously anxiety provoking. I told the doctor of this and he said whilst the blackouts are physical, there is evidence of this, the tiredness and exhaustion could be mental, related to a creeping up of depression. He has said he wants me to see my psychiatrist again to be reassessed to see if I am again clinically depressed as this could be a major symptom. But I have been clinically depressed for over ten ears and it has never felt this way. I have never been physically weak with it, unable to move my arms or legs. I have not wanted to, but this isn't at all the same feeling. I can see his point though, so I agreed, and said I would seek my GP and ask if he felt I needed anti depressants again and also to see if he could look into this weakness. It has been suggested I may be suffering from a form of ME, although I hesitate to say this, and think it, until a physician thinks this is the case.

I have to be careful not to let my imagination run away with me, as I have stated, I can get pretty obsessive. But I feel inside that something is wrong, physically, and as depressed as I may be, it could be the physical stuff that's causing it not the other way around. However I am not an expert in neither the mental health nor physical health fields, so I shall leave it upto those who know to decide. But I shall be sure to tell them everything, and to keep an open mind.

This is all making going to my voluntary work extremely hard, I can't focus when im there, I frequently feel like im going to blackout even when I don't, I manage to catch up quite well, but I am not able to give my best, and its interfering with my life and with my recovery. With the person I wish to be. That's something I want to explore, here and now. What do I want to be known for? Who do I want to be, what qualities do I want to cultivate within me? I want to be true to my beliefs certainly, I wish to be a follower of Christ, trying to have his grace, his compassion. Although I will fail, as I am imperfect, I have to try. So what do I long to be?

I long to be very much stronger. Stronger and steadfast and loyal. a source of strength and light. I long to be a giver, not a taker, as I am currently. A sapper of will, stealer of strength. This is not who I desire to be. I desire to be, and to be seen as, an intelligent, talented soul, who listens and understands, a soul who is loved by others, and who knows how to love in return, a source of competence and reliability, exuding confidence and self esteem, instead of being the incompetent and insecure wreck that I am currently. I long to look in the mirror, and like what I see, to like the person reflected back at me, amongst the light. I want to look at myself, and be able to say truthfully, yea, I have value, and even more, to know, without a shadow of a doubt that I am valued, and that it is justified.

I do not want to be a leader of men, or to be looked up-to, I need no pedestal, want no admiration, I want only to be looked across to, to be acknowledged as an equal, with my own talents, I want not to be led, but to be walked along with, side by side, in whatever venture I partake. Wherever my life may take me.

I wish only to be recognised as an individual, to be respected as such, to be cherished as a valuable member of whatever team or community I find myself in. I want to be included as an equal, not someone who should be included for decency's sake, but as one, who belongs, is needed, and valued. And wanted, I want my inclusion to be a natural thing, like breathing and passing urine. And in return, I will work hard, and prove that I deserve this respect. Deserve the respect I am given, I will show that I can give something in return. I want only to belong, but I want my belonging to be real, not forced. I want to feel that I have value, that as a person, I am worthwhile.

I cannot find any meaning in the life I lead, I cannot find any meaning in whom I am, I have searched my soul, read philosophy, and some existentialism, studied Buddhism, and still I cannot find the reason, for which I am here. Since I have become a Christian life makes a bit more sense, that god has his plan for me, and I will never fully understand it as we can never fully understand God. And because I believe in God, my heavenly father, I think we are all here for a purpose, we must be. I cannot have gone through all I did as a child, the bullying, the abuse, the constant brow beating for nothing. And I cannot have survived the being left alone to fend for myself with no support for years, for no reason. I cannot accept that I am born only to suffer and die. There must be some deeper purpose to life some secret of the universe, some cosmic significance to each single human life.

And I need to know that there is at least a purpose for our species, to allow me to continue. I feel that my life is meaningless, and without reason. And the only way I can continue to justify my existence, is if we are needed for some purpose. And I can help others in some capacity or other, or by at least searching for this spiritual, and philosophical truth, this mythical answer, to the deepest question- "who, and why, are we?" Why does the bible say that if you commit suicide and die, it is a sin, and you will go to hell, that you shall be cast out, not saved, that you will not ascend to the kingdom of heaven?

Why would a holy book state such a thing, why would it make such a claim, if there wasn't some reason for each and every human life? Some complex and unfathomable reason for our existence as a species? If our lives were not important, and needed for some comic happening, why would such an act be forbidden? Perhaps this is the reason I struggle so much with being a part of society, and people.
Why I struggle so much with understanding them, and their motivations, is because I am not meant to be with them, that, their life, one of the moral majority, is not for me.

Could it be that's not to be my fate, not my destiny? Perhaps this is the reason I struggle so much with being a part of society, and people, understanding them, and their motivations. Is it perhaps because I am not meant to be with them, that, their life, one of the moral majorities, is not for me, that' it is not my fate, not my destiny? Perhaps I should lead a more hermetic existence, learning from boos, and travelling, visiting places such as Stonehenge. Learning about myths and legends, philosophy and religion… perhaps mine is a monastic calling, far from people and society.

Perhaps I just do not belong in the everyday community, I may be hard wired not to fit in, and perhaps I am just too different. Maybe it's a fault in my make up. Some neurological dysfunction that makes it so bloody hard for me to comprehend everything. Comprehend life, meaning, the world, people, myself. Everything. It has been suggested, put to me, it could well be because of the dyslexia. And because I am dyscalculic. And suffer from Dysphraxia to a certain degree. All of these things combined could add up to why things are so hard fro me to savvy, to work out, to comprehend.

It could also be that the fact I was bullied so badly, abused. Mistreated, they could all be factors that my personality make up is as it is. These are all possible reasons why I find just being, just sitting, so difficult, why integrating and being a part of things feels so insurmountable, so impossible for me. That this could be the reason I am so insecure and paranoid. That I am so difficult sometimes and why things are so difficult for me in return. I just get so confused, and I feel so stupid, so insignificant, and so un-normal, so mind bendingly stupid, dim, incapable of making sense of the madness that surrounds me, that I would be doing everybody a favour, me included, to just up and leave, and withdraw from conventional life forever.

The question is however, would I find acceptance amongst those, who too, felt they had no place in modern society, or would I jostle their nerves? Just as I do those in the mainstream world! And would I become an unwanted addition to a community that had no desire, for the likes of me? Would I be making a tremendous mistake? To give up what I have here, a flat, good friends, the support of a fine organisation, with lovely, lovely people looking out for me? And supporting me? Would I be ruining my life by taking the risk? Would I be ruining my life by taking such a notable risk? And how would I know? Or is fear of change, of making a mess of things the only thing that is stopping me making a move, and finding my place in the scheme of things? Making a contribution to a community that needs me? Is the very fact that I am considering such a course of action, an indication, that this is the only way I could be truly happy? Should I just accept my nature, go with my instincts?

 Trust in my belief that I do not belong here, that I should seek out some enclave of souls that have turned their backs on this life, forever, looking instead to the seeking out of glorious, glowing, truths? Should I seek counsel, advice and aid from those with clearer minds than my own, those neutral and level headed? Is that the move I should make? Or should I just make the decision and go, commit to a course of action, instead of trembling and shivering like a child? Should I be strong willed, and decisive, or more thoughtful, considering each possible outcome, identifying why I feel the need to go? Could it be that I am running from myself, or answering the call of something greater than I?

Who can say? Perhaps I should first examine what communities and groups are out there, visit the monasteries and the communities. Speak to the Buddhists and the Benedictine monks, speak with the elders of some of theses splinter groups, learn from them, why they live the life that they do. Maybe research is the key. I must fit in with one of these enclaves of the lost, somewhere. I must belong somewhere. I know I am a Christian so if this was the course I took; it would be in that sense.

But I at least know this. I must leave here, this place, this city, and do it soon. I have outstayed my welcome, and this city I live in strains to eject me, like I am a virus, being ejected from a body, immune system destroying me strand by strand. Ejecting me like so much refuse, so much waste.

But where will I go? I do not know. I have a destiny to meet, and a fate to find, I know not where, but I know I cannot continue here. My soul screams for release, and so I must go, as my heart calls me to action. Perhaps then, I can outrun this pain? Who knows?

I want to live a good life, to explore, to find my rightful place within this world, learn who I am, and what I am meant to be. I can only do that by going "walkabout" I feel, simply put, just picking a direction, and going, just going. Without fear, without hesitation, headlong, into my future. And I need to do this fairly soon I think, to protect whatever sanity I have remaining to me. It's funny what we will do, in the hope of escaping agony, isn't it? I really want to escape to be loved, to find meaning.

And so it really is that simple. I want true love to come my way, and I really want to be completely wish to be prepared for it when it does. I have made a decision, to leave the single life behind me, and so I am now actively looking for a partner. So yes, I want someone, and as I am bisexual, gender is not an issue for me, as it is for many of my fellows. It is the heart, the soul that attracts me, not just the flesh, so no matter which gender that someone is, if they touch me inside, then they are right for me.

Like I have already said, I am somewhat of a romantic, and I believe true beauty comes in many forms. It matters not which gender. Be it male, female, transgendered, it's all the same to me, true love knows no bounds, and there is no barrier to my heart. My Sexuality is not fixed. I am attracted to men and women, and men who used to be women, and vise-versa, it is purely what's inside that matters to me. Clichéd, I know, but true nonetheless.

This is something I have spent many sleepless nights over, many days without eating, lots of heartache and run in's with folk coz of it. I was sure I was gay when I was 20 or so, it took months to come to that conclusion, but I did. Then I was about 25, when I thought I appreciated the female form, and started thinking about going with a woman (I had slept with men, but never women) then I decided I was bi-sexual. I have never felt I was straight, and I still don't. I have come to realize that it's natural for me to b able to see beauty in both the male and female form. Indeed, that the real beauty is that person's soul, what's inside…?

And it's that I am really attracted to. I appreciate both that and the physical form that comes with it. I no longer feel a need to identify in any way, I just am, and I am me. But when necessary, when I need to apply a label, it's the one of bisexual I relate to the most. I love men and women for their beauty both internal and external, it's the personality that calls to me, and flesh and bones are secondary. We are after all not just bags of skin…

Because of that, I see it as very strange that people hate each other due to sexual orientation. It seems barbaric and underdeveloped to not be able to see that attraction isn't only linked to bodies. Pheromones, vibes, personalities, these all have a part to play in attraction, so to hate someone because they are gay, bisexual, or lesbian, or transsexual or transgendered, then that is to me bizarre. I can only hope there are others with the same way of seeing the world, or at least similar. That there are others with my particular orientation, and that I happen across them, some day, somehow. I hope, against all hope that I will find someone out there, amongst the streets, the roads and byways that make up this nation.

Not only do I want a partner, I want to have friends, and people who respect me for whom I am. I am not sexually attracted to either the male or the female form. I seek a hug, closeness, intimacy, affection, but I do not seem to want sexual encounters. Maybe this is not normal I know not. The fact is at 26 years of age I am still a virgin, and I may die one. I care not I assure you. I want only love. But it's beginning to feel like that's something I shall never have. I feel a pain at the core of my being. I am feeling the pain of separation. I feel as if I am separated from the love that is the heart of living beings, love of god, love from god, from our fellow beings... it simply just hurts.

And it's funny, that although it hurts. I hurt, I am clearer minded and more optimistic, then I have ever been before.... I guess I know more now. I am going to overcome my issues whatever they be, whether they are these physical ones, the mental ones I have long struggled with, new challenges, whatever.

I will persevere, I am stronger, I have found faith, I have good people in my life again, different ones, but good for all that. Perhaps I will find my release in spirituality; perhaps I will end my journey, at least for a while, by spending time in a rural commune, in some part of Britain. Or some community, or monastery, or such like. The opportunities for self discovery are endless, limited only by my imagination, determination, and strength of will. I do find myself strongly attracted to Stonehenge, as if I am being called there by a higher power, a force beyond my reckoning, drawing me exonerably onwards....

Truth or fantasy, who can say, who is qualified to quantify the unknown? Certainly not me, and if you feel you are, you are a better person, than me, my friend. I guess we are all strangers in a strange land. We are all travellers on a voyage of discovery, travelling the roads of wisdom and discovery. Who knows? Maybe we shall pass by, like ships in the dark night, or perhaps we shall meet, by the campfires of need, and necessity, perhaps we will come across each other. I must say, at this point, that the thing that has made this journey tolerable for me, upto the point of writing this, is the people I have come across. My volunteer work at the Llgbc, my associations at network for change, people I have met at cell and my church, all have helped me immensely. I am bisexual, and my community has been a great help to me. All of the seriously cool people I have met in my life, have helped so, so much, coz I feel I have learnt a little from each of them.

Not all of it has been pleasant. Some of them were enemies, who later became friends, once I worked out why they didn't like me so, some stayed as antagonists, and I learnt from them too, in my way.

In some cases, there were acquaintances, and in some cases, very good friends, and through them, I feel I have learnt compassion, kindness, the ability to be gentle, but strong. (I feel arrogant saying this, but it is nevertheless, true) and I have also received much in the way of friendship, and a feeling of acceptance. Well I did. That state of being is a little rocky, right now. I hadn't ever felt that way before, and on reflection, it feels like a ray of sunlight, piercing thick, heavy, bilious cloud

 I am a seeker, and that's what I must do, keep on searching, looking, one day, I may even find what I am looking for. But perhaps it isn't the destination that matters, its how you get there. As well as everything else I have said up to this point, I have discovered, I do have fixed goals, things I yearn to achieve. Yeah, strangely I have found this is actually the case. During the process of writing this book, things have changed and evolved for me. So that above and beyond what I have explored with you, I do have things I enjoy, although its only been through writing this book, that I have come to recognise them, and be able to enjoy them.

It isn't perfect though. My ability to focus and enjoy stuff is not what it should be. Not fully, not yet, but I am beginning to relax a little more I feel, taking it slowly, slowly, I guess. Well, where do I start? It feels kind of odd reeling off good stuff, but here goes.

I really like my music, and films, because they express other peoples visions, ideals, desires, and I feel like they are speaking to me, revealing something about their spirits, and I learn more about the world and myself, through those medias. My favorite music is by the following bands/groups/Artists, The cure, Echo and the bunnymen, the smiths, Lou Gramm, Roger Daltry, Tim Cappello, blink 182, the coral, the police, Frankie goes to Hollywood, the streets, Franz Ferdinand, haircut 100, spiritualized, the shaman, linkin park, motley crue, the offspring, pantara, soulfly, miles Davis, bob Marley and the wailers, boomtown rats(introduced to sir bob, by a friend, whom I have lost contact with unfortunately), green day, public enemy, turbonegro, skindred, Korn, Bach, Beethoven, enya, clannad, the fugees, NIN, Marylyn Manson, the Farm, the pixies, Nirvana, weezer, fear factory, plus -44, velvet revolver, Eddie and the tide, Goldfrappe (listened to a mates stuff, really liked it, thought I would hate it, but its cool.)

 Bauhaus, sioxie and the banshees, joy division, new order, Deacon blue, Bill withers, pet shop boys, go west, scarlet division (sad but true! – sundial is ace!) Static X, Goldie lookin chain, Ah-ha, nick cave (and his various bands), Black flag/ Henry Rollins (I love liar.), bad religion, smashing pumpkins, at the drive in, KYUSS, Red hot chilli peppers (obviously, what's not to like?), metallica, System of a down, black Sabbath, madness, velvet underground (some of their stuff, haven't heard a lot of it, I admit) INXS, mummy calls, Thomas Newman, Gerard McMann, murder dolls, Amen, stone sour. Level 42 (I am getting into dodgy territory here, I know), beastie boys, Disturbed, Gary Newman, Leftfield, QOTSA, foo fighters.

And many others – I have an eclectic taste in music, to say the very least! And I think this is somehow fitting. With such a wired personality, it's a relief to find I am a bit mixed up in my music tastes as well! Music for me, leads onto other media, like film. So what are my favorite films? Glad you asked (And if you didn't ask, I will tell you anyway, since I am an annoying git).

Bowling for columbine, (for the obvious reasons),Equilibrium (Very 1984/ Fahrenheit 451 like, but with emotions controlled, not knowledge, or behavior so much, though that's obviously part of it), Gangs of new York (I learnt a lot about History here, the Irish immigrants, the trouble they faced, the riots, the violence – very illuminating), Priscilla, Queen of the desert (Dragqueens, crossing a dessert, being proud, with dignity, whilst battling bigoted rednecks, what's not to like?),

 K-Pax (this is a film focusing on catatonia, (the problem, not the band! Chuckle) and more general Mental Health issues such as Loss of reality, dissociation, paired with a sci-fi plot, and aliens from an other dimensions who exist in energy forms – very thought provoking), the crow, the crow2, Labyrinth, Drop dead Fred, beetlejuice (all three of these really effected me growing up, it made me feel wonder, let me let my mind slip free, dream, imagine – they saved me pretty much. Kept me sane.),

 big Trouble in little china (this was the first ever martial Arts film I ever saw, and it blew me away, made me want to watch more, which eventually led to me taking martial arts lessons as a teenager). More recently, Revolver,(Guy Ritchie is a dude of a man) Band of Brothers, Knight Watch,

A history of violence (David Cronenberg coming back to full strength!) All of this made me feel, which is unusual for me, these days – to be moved by a movie. Which is as far as I am concerned the mark of a good film. I actually was moved by the plots of these. God, I love the Cinema! Oh, and being the Sci-fi fan I am, I loved Serenity (the big screen spin off from firefly) even though I never watched more than a few episodes of firefly.

Of course there is a little more to me than music and film. (As I have so recently discovered, or should I say, rediscovered, perhaps?) I read some philosophy, because I want to know how others think, and I am very interested in the concepts of morality and ethics. What is moral? What's ethical?

I think it's different for everyone, and it all depends on your cultural context. I prefer eastern stuff, to western philosophy; I feel I relate more to an eastern mindset some how. I also love to write; as it lets me express myself, in the way those others do via film and music. I write a lot right now, firstly more about me, Semi-autobiographical, like the book you are now holding in your hot and sweaty little hands.

But most of it is not like this at all. Now it is much more fictional, about people making big decisions, in a weird and surreal kind of way. I enjoy that a lot. I also write poetry, its not great stuff, but it does give me expression, release, so that I can go my way, get on with my life. It's a kind of safety valve.

 I also like to draw, I used to draw still life, then peoples faces, then simplified cartoon versions of real people, now I am moving into anime, which is great, but challenging. Learning to draw with in another cultural context is difficult, I am also trying to learn to draw in the marvel, DC, mold – super-hero's, villains etc.

I used to be really into computer hardware years ago, and tech generally, and I am beginning to get an interest again. So we will have to see how that develops in the next year or so.

I used to bungee jump; I did four very close together, joined a bungee club, never did it again, and I would like to take it up again, reawaken that devil-may-care approach again. I also wish to learn to wind-serf, and rock climbing. Both of which are possible, nearby. My last real desire right now, is to learn the saxophone; I played the trumpet, years ago whilst at school, but didn't really like it. But saxophones, wow… the sounds that emerge really inspire me, make me feel. There is so much to me, so much I am rediscovering again.

I really am beginning to feel real for the first time in years. Recovery is looming on the horizon, and I am walking out to meet it. That being the case what else is on my mind? What else do I long for? I really want to travel, see Egypt, the sphinx, the pyramids. I want to swim with mountains, I want to go and see New Zealand, both the north and south islands. I want to visit Australia, have a year out there, work there, sleep under Ayer's rock, and see the outback, the bush! I want to be a writer; I want to see as much as I can, do as much as I can, live as much as I can, whilst I can. I am open as to how I get there, no real plans, I just want to do it. I believe I can, and will, but it will take time, money, and the right mind state. Hey, since I want to be a writer and am working on my first book

right now (other than this one, duh!!) I would like to share a couple of extracts with you of it with you.
"The first is called in he walked."

"In he walked."

"He walked in like he owned the joint,(which he did, being strikingly rich) swaggering up to the reception desk, with a self -satisfied smirk on his face, dressed expensively, and smelling like cash. He exuded charisma, and left you feeling dirty and inadequate. He was one of those smug bastard, Hollywood movie types, good looking, and indecently so. And he knew it, using that knowledge to his advantage. He could have bought and sold the bank several times over, and still have money left over for a coffee, and that was just out of his pocket change. The name on his pocket book said Jebidiyah h. shanks.

You could tell his pleasure at this state of events from across the bank, sickening you with its potency. There was something sleazy and rotten about him, leaving you with a crawling sensation across your skin. There was something odd about the fella tough, something about the cast of his expression, eyes wide and unfocussed, glassy, and cold, a manic grin passed across his face, remaining there, frozen. He was covered in sheen of perspiration, heat coming off him in waves. His face was red and puffy. He was evidently not well, for all his cash and fancy clothes, something, was just not right. You could sense it.

And this perception was proven correct, when without warning, he dropped to his knees, with a demonic wail, swaying about, Braying, as he laughed hysterically, sounding for the entire world, like a deranged hyena. Madness glinted in his eyes, along with something darker, more sinister. All movement stopped, as if a switch had been clicked into place, as heads swiveled to check out this sudden disturbance, with a sick curiosity. His laughter changed pitch in tone, becoming more strident and shrill, until it was no longer recognizable as coming from a human throat. It erupted like some kind of animal scream, a piercing scream of pain and terror, like something from a third rate horror movie,

Where the victim stands frozen by fear, as the creeping death advances forwards, not needing to rush, not slowed down in the least, by the persistent, constant screams of the poor doomed innocent. But this was no harmless movie, no escape from reality here. No, this was harsh unyielding reality, frighteningly real, the scene of a mysterious and spectacular breakdown, the site of a mind retreating from reality, to inhabit some strange, shadowy, internal dimension, from which it might never return.

He laughed, and he kept laughing, harder, and harder still, shaking more and more violently, until suddenly, he was still. He lay there, staring blankly at the wall, lost to reality, lost to the people milling around him. Gazing down onto his prone and fragile form, gone was its charisma now, gone was the immense force coming from him, as if it had never been there at all. There was no life in his face at all. But behind his eyes, lay a silent scream, as he was beset by forces beyond the ken of normal human experience.

This was no normal collapse, if such a thing existed. No, this was an intrusion by some external force; this was the result of a mind being shared, against its will, by a stronger, more dominant, Life force. The religious would come to view this as demonic possession, and on the face of it, this was true, but the demons were not terrestrial in origin. Though this was indeed a possession. They had chosen a rich figurehead, a man of power, with the ability to cow with his commercial might, and it was no coincident that the seemed breakdown came in a bank, a place of wealth. A place of power.

It was a breakdown; it was the death cry of a spirit surrendering control to its abuser, its nemesis. It was a demonstration, and attempt to reach into the human physke, to dominate them, to show that even those who were powerful can fall and be made to bow. The now completely dominated Movie guy sat up, and climbed lithely to his feet. He brushed himself off, chuckling to himself in a wry tone, tutting at his fall. He removed his sunglasses, to reveal churning forces of electric blue, where his pupils should have been.

He grinned, and the temperature of the bank dropped by a few degrees. You could sense the malignancy in the air, the oppressive power coming from him." Attention please. My name is Jebidiyah," He paused for effect, before going on." I have an interesting announcement to make, he began." "Human kind has had its day of glory, its fifteen minutes in the sun, and what have you done with them? You have wasted them, warring amongst yourselves, dividing the rich against the poor. You should have killed the poor, the weak.

 You should have dominated your lessers, and taken your wrath to the stars, but you didn't. You attracted the attentions of your betters instead. There are no second chances.

You are weak. We are strong. We will dominate you. You will change your lifestyles to service us. That's all. Have a nice day". Jebidiyah or at least the malignancy that now wore his face knew they would hear from him again. This was just the beginning. He smiled a highly unpleasant smile, and calmly left the building, looking for a place to begin. All around the world, similar events were occurring, as humanity was given its final notice. It s tenancy of earth was about to come to an end, and they were being evicted. The invasion had begun.

And so Jebidiyah Shanks became a figure of great importance. His financial backing would make all later events possible. He was truly the fulcrum, on which the fate of the earth was balanced. So, we know that New York was visited by the Shakara, the foul force we would come to know and fear as Anti-life, but what of the rest of the world? What was afoot? Where were they, and how would they announce their presence to us?

In England, Karl ran, ran as if his life depended on it, which of course it did. Oh, how it did. It was 1984, in more ways than one, the book, had become the reality, a harbinger of the doom that was to follow, freewill no longer free, free expression, now just a wild dream. Thoughts and dreams were monitored, and speech of any kind, was allowed only to the rich and powerful. The penalty for speaking even a single constenant, or vowel, was death. The means of that death depended on how much you spoke, how badly you had broken the law. And so it was entirely up-to you.

Karl had spoken out, spoken out against the regime, against the illuminati, he had challenged the way of things, in the media, on the street, and he was hunted.

He had done the unforgivable. He had had an original thought, voiced it, and shown himself to have personal power. And this was unacceptable. England was a country dominated by politics, and politics were dangerous, lethal. Nobody spoke the truth (indeed, most people did not speak, period)

Honesty was a thing of the past, false cheesy grins and stoic hearts were the only safe way of expressing yourself, inner thoughts were concealed desperately, so the police could not see them. They had hearts of steal, and souls that were black and corrupted. England was a dictatorship, , controlled by the Prime minister and his lackeys. George bush was but a memory, Tony Blair, lost to history. Saddam Hussein a legend. Alqaidea had been erased from the history books.

It had happened suddenly, almost overnight. The pm had been replaced by force; the military had backed a mystery man, who once in power, drastically changed the balance forever. Democracy was now little more than a fancy title, all style, no substance. It no longer existed. No one would believe that this momentous change for the worst, this loss of civil liberty, this heinous crime against the British population, was orchestrated by the unknown, an alien race who were bent on the destruction of all life in the galaxy.

The anti-life had awoken here ten sweet years ago, and had slowly subverted the political processes here, finding a way into our hearts and minds, and clenching them, as if in a steel vice. Evil shows itself in many forms, and the Shakara are no different. So they had ensnared us.

England was once again the head of a global empire, and all suffered in her embrace. Politics had gone mad, and the justice system no longer resembled the thing it had once been. The police was run by the mafia; parliament was an open arena, where the innocent and powerless were put to death, and the lords and ladies, watched with baited breath.

Heckling was punishable by death, as was littering, gathering in groups, being out after 5.30pm. You left the compounds to work. After work, you returned to the compounds, and you ate and slept. Anything else was treasonous and punishable by death. There was no prison system, as there were no prisoners. All crime had one punishment, death.

The only difference was in how painful that death would be, and that depended on how much trouble you gave the regime. Political manifestos were the new bible, parties vying against each other, though behind the scenes, they all wanted the same thing, they all supported each other, they were the same party. They were the new monarchy, and the king, was the PM. Mp's were the priests of a new kind of religion, all religious ministers of any kind had long since been put to death, for public nuisance citations. "Arousal of the public".

The party political broadcast had evolved, it was law, it was education. It was how to think, dress, act, how to speak. How to be. Each new child was assigned a role in accordance with the needs of the regime. If they failed, they died. And a new vacancy was filled. Again and again. If you did not take part, if you did not live as you were told, if you did not do your job well, you became a political refugee. Hunted down, and exterminated, wiped out, erased from history.

Most did no try to run, they ere taught a children not to. If you failed, you were "recycled" so that society could prevail. It was brainwashing to accept your death, so the regime didn't have to expend resources to chase you down.

If you ran, you died more painfully. But at least you had a chance to live, live a real life, one of free will. Most did not remember what that was like, and so, did not miss it. People were mindless automatons, existing only to do the jobs to keep the country aloft. They were only a means to power. Smarminess and twaddle now were the official language, the moral majorities were no longer moral, peace was just another name for war, and the world was decked out in the colors of political parties, red, green, blue, and yellow. The colors you wore identified your position in society. These bright and gaudy colors belied the dark, grimness of reality in which Karl lived.

If only he could escape over the border, into Wales, where they were free, wild, pagan, and strong. They had fought, they had not succumbed… representatives of the English regime had gone to Wales to negotiate, to gain power, without overt military action, certain that thinly veiled threats would be sufficient to force a change. But the delegates had not returned. At least, not all of them. Their heads however had made it back to number 10.

And so it was to Wales that Karl ran. Death perhaps awaited him there, but it was better than remaining here. Pausing only for breath, Karl ran, he ran, as if his life depended on it, which it did. Oh, yes. It certainly did. Karl did not know whether or not he would be safe, Wales had dropped out of contact 9 years ago, to this day, actually. They had pulled out, disgusted with the processes in action. All attempts to enter had been dealt with force, and in fact, England had never really tried. But he would. He had no choice at all. He would make a difference. He had to."

"Children of the Flame"

"And so, We all stood, swaying, dancing around the fire, passing through the thick plumes of smoke, inhaling burning sage, cleansing us of our past, as we were celebrating our pagan roots, watching the embers as they smoked, and we worshipped the blessed elements, and we were reborn, as if a phoenix from the flames, young and vibrant, strong and free. This was our ritual, every year we met, on this day, for the festival, basking in the glow of the flames, reveling in the sweat dripping from our bodies, making us slick, as we passed through the smoke, loving its smell.

As we turned, danced, swayed our way ecstatically through the night, as if in a trance, guided by some unseen force, our uncertainties turned to ashes, and the power of our desire, burned within us, like fiery hot coals. There was much cheer, a feeling of shackles dropping away, as we watched the fire eaters doing their thing, after they had ignited the torches with petrol, showing no fear as they inhaled the life giving flame, the genesis of mankind.

 Eventually, the rituals drew to a close, and we ended with a wonderful fireworks display, which signified, to us at least, taking old values into a modern future, the fireworks left the air heavy with the smell of sulphur, strong, and putrid, the smell of brimstone bringing to mind the Christian view of hell, which we quashed immediately, as that was not for us, we belonged to an earlier, more primitive time, and we were powerful, in perfect harmony with the life giving force of nature.

For tonight at least, we were what we should have been. After this passed, we sat and chatted, and watch the sky change, as it brightened, going from brown, to dark blue, to grey as day broke once more, the start of a new day, and a new beginning.

The bonfire stood smoking and crackling, a reminder of the night before, the night we were reborn, at the festival of fire, as children… of the flame.

This would be our banner, our motto. The children of the flame would protect hat was ours. We would protect the world, as from now on, nationality, color, creed, beliefs, none of this mattered. We were human, one race, and one species. One world. Against an insidious threat, one which we could not see could not predict. We could trust no-one, and yet we needed all, to survive."

So there they are. A couple of extracts from what I hope will be my next book "From Whence they came".

Writing is something that burns within me, I want to it so badly; it seems the only thing that keeps me sane and well, when everything else fails me. This is what I want.
Saying that though there is something I want above all of this, as long as it is in line with God's goals for me. I have an Ultimate Goal – Dream

And you know that it isn't complicated at all? Do you know that it is deceptively simple?

To be an ambulance Technician, saving lives, working with the old, the fragile, those needing care, to chat and support those needing my strength. This is not going to happen right now, as I have these blackouts and you cannot learn to drive till you are safe on the road, till the illness is controlled, and you have to not have a blackout for a year before you are allowed on the road. And you also need to be able to drive, and have a clean driving license for at least two years before you can join the service. I cannot drive, so I have at least three years to wait before that becomes possible. But that gives me three free years to give of myself. To work for amnesty and CND and Christian aid in my spare time Helping others working to bring about a world where we are all equal and as one. To carry on doing stuff for the Llgbc

What else do I want then? To live on a river boat/Barge, traveling the canal system, me and my cat, maybe a dog too. I want to be able to Travel from place to place. Experiencing life fully and being in the drivers seat not just a passenger as I am right now. I had a heart stopping thing happen recently. I think its one of the things that will stay with me throughout life, one of those moments where you know you could have changed course. It was a crossroads moment. One of those what if? Points we all go through.

I had a chance to make my dream of the canal boat life true and real recently. But I passed it over. Knowingly, and perhaps correctly, but I still find myself morning that lost chance. Let me explain. I live in Leicester, and my brother lives in Syston, near a place called Watermead Park, a fantastic area stretching for miles and miles connecting Birstall to

Thurmaston and system and for miles. You can reach my area from there along the canal, and I live a long way from there. The canal runs through Watermead Park, and along there is a marina, the Thurmaston marina. My brother has an elderly friend known as "Paddy" (not his real name, obviously) who due to age and the bitterness of the last winter, has decided to leave the boat life, and move to Manchester to be with his son and nephews, in their house. He wanted to be a part of a family again after so many years of being alone. It is a positive move for him. This leaves his boat empty, and the option became available for me to pay him for it, and take it as my own.

My breath halted, time slowed down… this was my chance. I was going to conquer the universe dammit!!! Hahaha I thought. My day has come. Yeah right. I should have known better. He only wanted 25000 grand for it, and I wanted it. Wanted it more than anything I had ever wanted before. So I promised to come up with five hundred pounds deposit and the rest by the end of this month (March 2006) I didn't know where I was going to get the money from, but I knew I would. I would because I had to. I would sell everything I had if necessary. I would get a job, right now. The agreement made, I and my brother walked away in silence. Mike then told me he intended to get a 2500 loan for me in his name which I would may him back 100 pounds per month. I said I didn't want that, but he said it was my dream and he knew how important that was to me. Since I was 11 I have wanted this over half my life and he had the means to make it happen and as my brother he wanted to do this for me. My heart brimmed with joy. For all our fallings out, he understood me and wanted to assist me. He was standing by me. No, better than that, he was standing with me.

It was going to happen. I really was going to own my own canal boat. Of course there were things we had not considered in our excitement. Luckily, my brother is of a much soberer disposition than I, and came to a realization that this was too risky, before I did. He slammed on his breaks and broke his concerns to me, gently. After a few days of tears, I came to see why and I agreed with him. It felt as if the dream was dead. It wasn't and is very much alive, but at the time I felt devastated. The reason we stopped the process will become obvious in a moment or two.

In his excitement to help me mike had forgotten speaking to paddy, and he telling my brother that the hull had started to leak sometime ago, and as paddy hadn't the money to have it hauled out of the water long enough to have a whole new bottom fitted they had welded a new flooring over it, and laid the floorboards over this. That would be ok, if the hull wasn't rotted and rusting, but it was. So basically, it is ok right now, but because of this new bit added, the air and water already inside would eventually oxidize and rust through, and the boat would sink lower and lower until eventually it flooded.

Paddy had been in it two years, but it wouldn't be many more before it was uninhabitable. Also it had no interior, just a floor. He had a wood burner a mattress in the corner a gas cooker on bricks, and that was it. So it is Hardly a prime buy. With every other expense added, license, British waterways fees, fuel costs, certificate of compliance, marina fees, it would cost over five grand, and I couldn't afford that. Or risk taking a full time job and relapsing at this point in time.

So mike talked me out of it. And we went to various marinas and found nice fully fitted boats for ten or 11 thousand pounds. So now I have a more realistic dream than I ever did before. I have set myself five years to get back to work and raise the sum necessary to buy a boat. It is doable, and I know it's attainable. So it more in reach than it was before. But it still hurt to realize I couldn't do this now. I think that's a lesson I had to learn. I had to learn Moderation and planning. Not rushing in blindly, building a home without laying down strong foundations. So whilst I want this, and want it badly, I know enough to know I can't rush it. So yes, I want to all of this,

But I want to do all of this very slowly, discovering new things along the way, deepening my life experiencing and spirituality along the way. I want to be a writer, a professional writer, writing as a living, selling my stuff to all and sundry, making a living to finance my life on the boat.

These are all aspects of me, my physke, my need to explore, both myself, and the world around me. I find myself Yearning to know, to feel, to understand. To be all I can be. This is all me. I want to be whole. I want to be complete. And as I have come to look at all of this, I have also explored more completely, the spiritual side of me too. I have already said I do have this spiritual side, but I would like to expand on this theme more fully. Religion is not something I ever really did identify with, in itself. I used identify with the spiritual feelings that can come from it, not with any institution that tells you how to think or act, or feel.

I still have issue with the Church since my abuser was a Christian, but i realize it is the person not the

Church who hurt me. That person abused their power. And that person was not a real Christian. Because they couldn't have known the grace of god, not and do that awful thing. It is true god will forgive everything, but that person wouldn't have needed to commit an act like that if they truly felt god's love and understood his commandments. True followers of Christ have compassion. My abuser had none. I fully understand and except she was probably abused herself and had suffered all manner of terrible soul destroying torture mentally speaking,

But this does not excuse passing this damage onto someone else. Don't people realize that they are doing one of the most reprehensible things conceivable? Destroying a Childs physke, disrupting their mental functioning, displacing a fragile sense of the world around them, and deranging a still forming personality? It's like wiping out all a person is and will be. I cant think of anything worse than the destruction of a mind, the violating of a spirit, the ruining of a body. Is there anything that bad? Murder is the only other crime I can think of, which fits into this category.

 I realize I am not being Christian by not being able to forgive, so I give t to god, and I ask him to forgive me for my lack of forgiveness and ask for his grace so that in time I will forgive and make peace with myself over this. At the moment that is the best I can do. And I truly believe that God understands this. I believe in Christ, his sacrifice, the heavenly father and his love for me, that is the important thing, not the building, not the symbol of my abuse. You know?

My mum decided not to have her kids baptized even though she was baptized and my grandma was a devout catholic. So, yeah, I was never baptized, as my mum wisely decided I should have free will, be free to choose my on destiny, so I looked about a bit, looked at Jehovah's witnesses, but disagreed with their philosophy in certain areas. Although having got to know them better I now am not so sure I disagree with everything they say. Indeed much of it appeals to me. But I don't know it is right for me. I don't know which faith is right for me. My love for god is solid, my belief in Christ Jesus complete. But that is all I know right now. I pray that god will show me the way. So I have looked around a lot, oh yes.

I looked at Confucianism, liked that better, liked Taoism even better, really related to Buddhism, having studied it for five years and I still do relate, I feel very close to this, spiritually, but I am also restless, I'm not a warrior, but I'm probably not monk material either. (Never did look good with a skin head, and since im a vegan, I wouldn't like a woolen robe either. Scratchy ass wool... why do they do it?)

I am so energetic, (Speedy Gonzalez and the road runner aint got nothing on me.)Not so calm, a bit aggressive, (I am like the nutty guy out of police academy, you know the one who screeches a lot) and the pagan traditions, the heathen traditions call to me, (the idea of bouncing around a camp fire muttering odd stuff is strangely appealing.. hey I am crazy, remember?) and right now, I am just reading up on as many of these as I can find, trying to see why people like them. This is maybe wrong believing in Jesus as I do. But there is nothing wrong with understanding other people's choices. I have made mine and intend to stick with it.

I am not looking for something, someone to guide me, no higher power, other than my god, the god of truth, the god of love, but a philosophy I relate to, one that i feel comfortable with, one I click with. (Feel the love, baby.)

iT may sound odd, but I am not ashamed of my sexuality, and as a Christian I quite often feel I should be. I admit, that through the writing of this book I have tried to suppress it, tried to cut off from my lgbt community, but that's stupid. I am proud of who I am, proud of my sexuality, my community and my friends. I love god, but I am bisexual, that is the truth of it. The Llgbc is such a huge part of my life, and I owe them so, so much. So I just want to say thanks a lot guys!

There it is. This is my story. I have told you my story, and I would (very much) like to hear yours. We all have a story to tell, and although I have no idea, who will read my little tale, whatever your experiences are, I would like to hear them, and add them to my own, increasing my knowledge, awareness, and humanity, assisting my growth. If you would like to share, I am delighted.

I must make one last statement before I leave you, thank you to every one who is or has been a part of my life.

I respect and admire you all, you have added to my character, made me better, more knowledgeable, a nicer, more rounded perhaps person. I am sorry for the times I have been an idiot, a git. I have not always acted as I should, and I deeply regret all of that. Thank you again; you all know who you are.

For those of you, who have left my life because of the hurt I have caused you, please know you are all so important to me, and I long to have you in my life again. I am just too scared to make contact. If having looked within you want me as a friend again, please call me! For the rest of you, for those friends I have not yet had the pleasure of meeting, please get in touch and share your tale.

I can be contacted at **adampick@msn.com** so please drop me a line. We are all interconnected, pack animals that we are, and we all pass through each others lives, I believe, whether in this life, or the next, or the one after that…

Well I think that is about me done, this time around. Like I said I believe we all cross paths someday, as we all have something to teach, and we all have something to learn. (blimey, that's a bit profound for four am in the morning, which it is here in Leicester, in England, on the tenth of march, 2006) so I hope we meet. Whenever. So why wait until the inevitable conjoining of paths? It will happen eventually anyway. So drop me an email!! Or a letter (postal address is at the back of the book)

And who knows? It may have, already.

In this life or the next.

(Queue the spooky music!)

Take care my friends, fare thee well, thank you for sharing in this journey.

Now I must go, and rest, sleep and recharge, for my future, awaits me. And I fear it will not wait long. And I imagine, it probably would take offence if I stood it up, leaving it, like a bride at the alter, whilst the groom legs it, (figuratively speaking) in the opposite direction, fleeing for his life. It's hard sometimes not to do just that.

And so I must go. I have made sense for so long I need to go and sleep for an hour or 48. it has been a pleasure, if you like the book great if you don't , then please don't come after me with a hatchet or something. I am a nice boy, you know. I am just a bit sensitive. Although I am perfectly able to deal with some criticism and a fairly well crafted email or so. So yeah, feel free to contact me. So, As the Russians say, dosevedanya. As we say, Farewell,

And I risk adding, God bless you all.

Adios. And thank you so much.

Adam Stuart Pick